Your 2 Minds

Using your mind to *transform* your life

Your 2 Minds

SUZANA MIHAJLOVIC

Published by
Hasmark Publishing, judy@hasmarkservices.com

Copyright © 2018 Suzana Mihajlovic
First Edition

No part of this book may be reproduced or transmitted in any form or by any means, electronic or mechanical, including photocopying, recording or by any information storage and retrieval system, without written permission from the author, except for the inclusion of brief quotations in a review.

Disclaimer

This book is designed to provide information and motivation to our readers. It is sold with the understanding that the publisher is not engaged to render any type of psychological, legal, or any other kind of professional advice. The content of each article is the sole expression and opinion of its author, and not necessarily that of the publisher. No warranties or guarantees are expressed or implied by the publisher's choice to include any of the content in this volume. Neither the publisher nor the individual author(s) shall be liable for any physical, psychological, emotional, financial, or commercial damages, including, but not limited to, special, incidental, consequential or other damages. Our views and rights are the same: You are responsible for your own choices, actions, and results.

Permission should be addressed in writing to Suzana Mihajlovic at your2minds@gmail.com
www.your2minds.com

Editor:
Sigrid Macdonald
Book Magic
http://bookmagic.biz

Cover and Book Design:
Anne Karklins
annekarklins@gmail.com

ISBN-13: 978-1-989161-12-8
ISBN-10: 198916112X

"Change happens from the inside out – it starts in your mind and it starts with you. Suzana's inspirational stories and common sense approach to making quantum leaps in your results make this book a guide for growth and improvement. Apply the principles and change your life. You won't ever look back."

    Bob Proctor, Master Success Coach

"What if I told you that this book could remove whatever obstacles you may be facing and could create a huge, yet positive, shift in your life? Purpose is a driving force behind who you are and what you do. Suzana has learned that simple truth through her own compelling experiences that she shares within the pages of this heartfelt and inspirational book. She will help guide you to discovering your purpose by teaching you some simple tools and techniques that you can apply to your own life. A must read for anyone wanting to change their life by changing their mindset."

    Peggy McColl, *New York Times* Best Selling Author

"I absolutely loved reading **Your2Minds** by Suzana Mihajlovic! If you think this book is about the conscious and subconscious minds… hang on, because there's a delicious twist! This book opened up my mind and heart to new possibilities that I hadn't even considered. Devour this book and enjoy the brilliant insights. Suzana Mihajlovic is a genius!"

    Brett Sampson, President, Sampson Consulting

"**Your2Minds** will make you have a deeper perspective on what goes on inside your head. It will force you to reflect on what you have done, look at what you are doing and have a vision for your future. Suzana gets you to write down your thoughts and answers to her questions forcing you to engage the mind at a deeper level and tell your subconscious mind that you are ready to make a change and take action. The exercises help you to connect, identify, and recognize what you need to do.

She shares her personal experience showing us how one must choose the path and want to change. We will have different voices trying to direct us. No one is exempt from having 2Minds but we must make the choice of which we allow to be the dominant mind and use it to transform our lives. "

    Makini Smith, Author of *A Walk in My Stilettos*

"In this inspiring, open-hearted, easy to follow book, Suzana engages us with her personal life experiences and strategies that have transformed her life. Through this book, she shares those insights and provides useful, practical exercises to challenge her readers to work towards their full potential."

Dr. Reenu Farrugia, Psy.D

"*Your2Minds* is a book you will devour. One to keep close at hand and to read and re-read.
If you absorb and implement the ideas and strategies that Suzana suggests your life and results will change beyond all recognition."

Karen Mullins Consulting, Principal, Karen Mullins Consulting

"This book will undoubtedly change the way you see, feel and deal with your mind and life. Discover your inner power now!"

Sheila Benton, Personal and Business Consultant

"*Your2Minds* is written like a conversation between you and a trusted friend. Suzana shows you how to draw more meaning, greater satisfaction, and profound purpose from your own life with knowledge that comes from a deep place of wisdom. A conversation that could prove to be a turning point to building your life in ways you barely dare dream about."

Monte Young, USAF Major (ret), Southwest Airlines Pilot

*This book is dedicated to my late Baba Nada.
By letting your own light shine, you allowed everyone who
came into contact with you to allow their light to shine.
I love you to eternity.*

Table of Contents

My Gratitude	9
Foreword	13
Preface: A Message of Gratitude to My Mentor, Bob Proctor	15
"Without you the Universe will be out of alignment."	
PART 1: EXTRAORDINARY LIVING THROUGH YOUR2MINDS	**19**
Introduction	21
Your Extraordinary Life Exercise	26
I Must Have Been out of My Mind	31
What is Your Mind Telling You About Your Dream?	37
What would you do if it was guaranteed you couldn't fail?	48
Your2Minds	51
Your2Minds exercise	56
The Conscious and Subconscious Minds	59
Changing your subconscious mind to benefit you	65
The 2 Voices in Your Mind	67
The 2 voices in your mind reflection	71
Being in 2Minds	75
Making a decision when you're in 2Minds	79
The Power of 2Minds Working Together in a Spirit of Harmony	83
The 90 day challenge	91
My2Minds – Experiencing Depression and Anxiety	95
PART 2: A YOUR2MINDS: A LIVED EXPERIENCE	**101**
Mentoring Your Mind	103
Baba Nada's Marvellous Mind	105
The Baba Nada let your inner light shine reminders	113
PART 3: STEPPING OUT OF YOUR MIND TO FIND OUT WHO YOU TRULY ARE	**127**
Let Your Deepest Light Shine	129
Afterword: The Your2Minds Mission	135
About the Author	141

My Gratitude

I have so much to be grateful for not only in making this book a reality but also in my life in general. I am lucky. Many people make my life more enriched, more joyful, fuller, and brighter. Although I cannot mention every single one of them here, my gratitude goes out to them all just the same.

Before I begin to acknowledge the people in my life, I would like to acknowledge the thing that made the most difference in my finally stepping out and finishing the book I attempted to write so many times, and that is Thinking Into Results; this program turned things around for me and so many of my clients. Thank you, Bob Proctor and Sandy Gallagher, for your brilliance in putting this program together. I am proud to be a Proctor Gallagher Institute Consultant.

First, I would like to thank my loving family. You have all stood by me through thick and thin, through celebration and pride as well as through my darkest periods and embarrassing falls. You deserve the first acknowledgement because of your unconditional love and support and all that you have guided me through and taught me. You have always been there and loved me even during the times that it was painful to be around me. Thank you.

I would like to acknowledge and thank my incredible partner. You have been my greatest support in writing this book. Your honesty and frankness always push me to be better and do better, to dig deeper into my potential and keep drawing out greater quality. Your support and belief in me never go unappreciated. You continue to inspire me every day by being the person you are. Thank you.

Peggy McColl, your belief in me to get the job done assisted me in opening my mind to allow my heart to speak the words that are in this book. You took me in, and having you by my side helped me finally accomplish my mission, my dream. My goal to write a book has been living inside me for over forty years, and without your guidance, it would probably still be only a dream that I would get to 'one day'. The importance of having a coach or mentor was proof in your dedication to my mission. Thank you.

To my nephews and niece – Stefan, Luka, and Sara. You bring joy to my heart and light to my world every day with just a thought. You are the lights of my life. Never allow your own deep inner light to dim. You are perfect in your own imperfection and never forgot you could accomplish anything you ever dreamed of if you were ready to keep working on your mind. I am so blessed and grateful to have you. Although you are no longer little, you are still Teta Suzy's bundles of joy.

To my dear friend (you know who you are). Your support of me and belief in me never cease to fail. I must be the luckiest person in the world to have such a dedicated friend that I find in you. I am blessed. Thank you.

To my godchildren – Milica, Milena, Marcus, and Ellie. Thank you for choosing me for your 'Kuma.' Words cannot say how much love and light you bring to my heart. Your light is incredibly bright it lights up my heart. Keep focused on where you are going because if your Kuma could do it, so can you. Thank you.

To the children in my life – Cassandra, Nicholas, Zalaika, Jaidan, Jordan, Connor, Mihail, Ava, Mila, Luka, Milan, Natalija, Arianna, Nick thank you for all that you contribute to me and the world. You too are my pure joy. Teta Suzy, or Kuma Suzy for some of you, believes in you, and I cannot wait to experience your beautiful achievements in life. Remember never to let your light be dimmed. Thank you.

To my dear friends and relatives, who are too large in number to mention here, but as a start, Vicky, Marina, Draga, Tanja, Sofija, Vesna, Mirjana, Sonja, Danijela, Toula, Suzana, Irene, Biljana, Luciana, Sue, Phil, Suri, Monica, thank you for sticking by me throughout the years, for your ongoing support and loyalty. Thank you for making my life so much more fulfilling. Thank you to my big cuz Olivera, I miss you but continue to be inspired by you, Sladja and Marina, always in my heart.

Thank you to my meditation teacher, Vicky. You light the world wherever you go; you uplift, and you inspire.

Thank you to my incredible Master Mind group and my accountability partner. You powerful women never cease to inspire me, to push me through my fear and to continue to believe in me and where I am headed. Karen, Di, Rachael, Jacqueline, and Sheila you are power forces taking on the world. Keep focussed, individually and as a group we are achieving higher heights. I am so excited about our next stage.

Foreword

Purpose is a driving force behind who you are and what you do. Suzana has learned that simple truth through her own compelling experiences that she shares within the pages of this heartfelt and inspirational book. She will help guide you to discovering your purpose by teaching you some simple tools and techniques that you can apply to your own life.

If you are yet to discover your purpose, there are lingering questions that are often in the back of one's mind that pop up. For example:

What is my purpose?
Am I truly happy?
Who do I want to be?
Am I living the life of my dreams?

What if I told you that this book could remove whatever obstacles you may be facing and could create a huge, yet positive, shift in your life?

I have been in the personal development business for many years and have spent many of those years learning about why we do the things we do and, furthermore, why we don't do many of the things we are capable of doing. Many people are aware that their lives are not all that they had hoped for and would like to change that, but very few are aware that we are set up for success by nature — we are all created with infinite potential.

I feel honored to be invited to write the foreword for this book. Suzana became a client of mine, and from the moment I met her, I knew she had the power to change people's lives. When we met she asked me, with tears in her eyes, if there was any way possible that she could write her book in seven days; my answer was a resounding "yes!" In those few minutes I spoke with her, I felt her passion for transforming the world and saw her enthusiasm as she talked about her big dream of sharing what she had learned.

Suzana has learned from the best, Bob Proctor, when she decided to become a Proctor Gallagher Institute (PGI) Consultant. The training taught her how to assist people with goals and shifting paradigms so they can have the success in life that they had always dreamed of having.

This book will enlighten you to discover your own path. Suzana has created an easy to use guideline for choosing goals that will improve your life, both now and in the future, and goals that fall in line with the person you are and want to be.

Success and happiness do not happen by accident. People create their own lasting happiness and success by creating positive habits, being disciplined, and choosing their thoughts and actions

> *"All you need is the plan, the road map, and the courage to press on to your destination."*
> ~ Earl Nightingale

There are many excuses that we tell ourselves that prevent us from being truly happy, and within these pages, you will learn how to move past them. Not only is the content incredible and highly-actionable, but the exercises and thought provoking questions at the end of each chapter will force you to dig deeper and make the positive change you desire.

Since we are on a constant quest to better ourselves and our lives, *Your2Minds* empowers you to do what you must to be your best you. The key is not to dwell on the past but rather take those lessons and apply them to your life today. Embrace your failures as experiences, and use them to motivate yourself to do better in the future.

Use this book as your road map to making changes in your life that you never thought were possible: the extraordinary power lies within YOU!

Peggy McColl
New York Times Best Selling Author

Preface
A Message of Gratitude to My Mentor, Bob Proctor

"Without you the Universe will be out of alignment."

*"I am a spiritual person living in a human body,
not a human body with a spirit."*
~ Bob Proctor

In order to succeed in life, every person needs a mentor. I am about to share with you an experience that I had with my mentor. This experience shifted my life in a profound way, and I would like you to open up your consciousness so that you too can have your own life-altering experience. When you truly open yourself up to the meaning of this, I hope that you will have a profound shift in your thinking about who you are, your life, and life in general.

Toronto, September 2017: I was sitting in a room full of people, and my mentor, Bob Proctor, said something along the lines of:

"Did you know that nothing in this entire Universe would move in the precise order it moves in your absence?.... Did you know that if you weren't here, the Universe would literally be out of alignment?"

Now there is something remarkable about this man. He is someone who completely lives what he preaches. Just having him in a room lifts the entire vibration, and when he says something, you can feel it resonate in every part of your body, on a cellular level.

As soon as Bob said this, my body almost convulsed. I felt it at the deepest of my core. It was like having his energy near me. Making this immensely profound statement about who I was allowed my energy to lift to a level where spirit was able to enter and do its work through me, within me. I have been around so many amazing people, but never has anything resonated in my life like this. It was certainly God, Spirit, the Universe, source or whatever you want to call it working its way through me.

Bob lived on this vibration. I do not doubt that the one hundred and fifty or so people in that same room also felt something shift inside them. The vibration was strong. One man in a room, with so many people, and that one man created a shift by lifting the vibration of the room to the level of his vibration.

This is enough proof for me, and all those who experienced it, that one man can change the world by changing himself first, by changing his mindset to function from a place of his infinite potential, through his spirit and deep inner light, his deep inner knowing rather than a place of fear, negativity, and a mind full of false images and viruses. Bob learned about his infinite greatness and changed his mindset and subconscious paradigms in his late twenties; he went from being in debt to being a millionaire in a very short period.

As remarkable a person Bob as is, he could not have transformed my thinking and uplifted my vibration on his own. I chose to open up and learn about who I was and what I could do to change my mindset so that I too could experience more of my infinite potential. I was ready, I was open, and for a long time, I wanted change. I had been working on "*Letting Go and Letting God*" for quite a few months before that experience. I craved that strong spiritual connection with source for most of my life and experienced it many times throughout my life. I worked hard on changing my deep embedded mindset and subconscious paradigms that were not benefiting me for a long time. This time, sitting about one meter away from Bob and hearing his words resonate to my deepest core, I felt as though I needed to allow myself be guided to the next step. I wanted so much more for myself and my life. I yearned to dig deeper and to unfold that infinite well of internal greatness. I prayed almost every day for guidance, and that day, I knew I was being guided.

Let me explain what Bob's words meant to me and why they affected me so strongly: we tend to undermine who we are to such a small and insignificant level that we are not using anywhere near our full potential, we are not even using a fraction of it actually. We often let fear and the negative messages we carry in our mind control us and make our everyday decisions for us. We pathetically think that we are not smart enough, not good enough, not beautiful enough, not worthy enough, not enough and on and on. We often allow others to give us these messages also. What we have missed, however, is that the Universe is an infinite, immensely and profoundly loving, immensely powerful, and creative force…and we are a part of that creation. The Universe created us. It created us through its love. It wanted us, and created every one of us as an intricate and irreplaceable part of itself through its omnipotent and everlasting love for us. So, if we are a part of that creation, our presence is critical in the bigger scheme of things so that the Universe can continue to function as a complete whole. Take one element out of the Universe, and it will not function in its natural alignment. Therefore, if we took you out of the Universe, the Universe would be out of alignment. Do you get it? If not, please go back and read that again.

Now if something hasn't moved inside you, I have not explained this properly, or you have not yet fully grasped what this means about your magnificence.

The above is my story, which for some reason, I am drawn to share with you. This book is for you and about you, so please, sit quietly for a few minutes, close your eyes, and say to yourself:

"Did you know if you weren't here, the Universe would literally be out of alignment?"

Say it again and again. Please do not get up until you feel it at the depths of your core. No matter what you have experienced, or the doubts that keep coming up, this is the truth. Now, I would like you to put your name in front of that statement, stand up, put your arms up in the air, and say it out loud:

"…(Your name), did you know if you weren't here, the Universe would literally be out of alignment?"

Now say it in front of your mirror. Write this statement down, and put it somewhere that you will see every day. Carry it with you because once you truly experience the truth of this statement, your life will never, ever be the same! There is nothing truer than this statement. Let it resonate. Do not read past this point until you feel it has resonated deep down into your core. Spend a day re-affirming this statement, and come back to this book, and read through it. There is nothing more important than you realizing this… not even finishing this book. It is the secret of how extraordinary you truly are. It is time to start changing your mindset so that you truly and deeply know your own worth, your own beauty and your own power. When your mindset changes and you understand and believe this truth, your life will change to match this truth.

Part 1

Extraordinary Living Through
Your2Minds

Introduction

*I*magine this scene for a moment.

You're sitting on the sofa in your lounge room relaxing. You think about getting up to go on your daily walk along the beach. As you try to move your body off the sofa, you notice that it is not responding. Your body feels a little fatigued and very heavy. Your body has been in great condition for many years, so you haven't felt this heaviness before. You try to get up off the sofa again, but the heaviness in your body keeps weighing you down. You sit there for a few seconds thinking how strange this is; you are confused as to why your body is responding this way. You try to jolt yourself up for the third time, but your body is still fatigued. You decide to lie down on the sofa for a while. As you're lying there perplexed, you try to relax. You're scanning your body in your mind trying to relax each of your muscles. Relaxation exercises have worked for you in the past as you have used them often. As you try to relax, you feel your legs exhausted and starting to ache. You try to move them, but it takes a lot of effort. This is strange as only yesterday your legs were functioning fine. You feel your bones crack as you, very slowly, start to move your feet first. You then focus on moving your legs again, and although they are aching, you slowly start to move them. It feels unusually difficult.

Outside it is a nice and sunny day. From where you are sitting, you can see through your favorite window in the house. Your round art deco window was one of the attractions that encouraged you to purchase your home many years ago. To this day, you love to sit by that window, watching the world go by, drinking your coffee, and reading your favorite authors.

It appears that there is not a cloud in the sky outside. You love sunny days and cannot bear to be indoors on such a beautiful day. Your heart wants to be outside; you really want to go for that long brisk walk on the pebbled sand at the local beach. That is one of your favorite things to do, to walk on the beach, listening to the sound of waves, feeling the pebbled sand under your bare, wet feet. You always dreamed of living by the beach, and this beautiful art deco home with the round window two blocks away from the beach was your ideal sanctuary. Being around water soothed you, the beach being your favorite place to be. It calmed your mind and nourished your soul. But today, for some reason, your legs are in pain. They are not cooperating with you. You will not be able to get yourself to your favorite place although you could do with a walk.

As you reach down to rub your aching legs, you notice your hand. It takes you by surprise. It looks old, wrinkly, and you have spots on it that you have never had before. You look at your other hand, and it too looks wrinkly. You are perplexed and are feeling a little panicky. What is happening? Something must be wrong.

With a lot more effort than usual, you support yourself up from the sofa. Your legs feel weak, but you are determined to get up. They feel like they are not your legs. As you get up and slowly start moving, you make your way to the bathroom. As you look in the mirror, your heart trembles. You are shocked and confused by what you see. The reflection looking back at you is not the one you are used to seeing. You shriek, "What has happened to me?" Staring back at you is an aged face with gray hair and hallowed eyes, wrinkly skin. You don't want to believe that it is you, but you know it is. Your eyes give it away. They are your eyes, the color, the shape. But they are missing something. The thing missing in them is that wonderful, youthful, cheeky spark that you have had in your eyes for most of your life. What has happened?! Your thick, shiny hair has turned completely gray, and it has thinned. Your plump cheeks have sagged too. Shocked, confused, perplexed, all emotions mixed into one, you do not know what to think or how to feel...As you stare into the mirror, your entire life starts to flash by you.

With a gasp of air, you wake up in a sweat, your entire body shaking. You wake up bewildered. For a moment, you don't know where you are. You look around startled, and you notice that you are in your bedroom. What just happened? You must have been sleeping, dreaming. "But how could it be a dream? That image in the mirror felt so real." it was you. You know it. You lie there in bed, not able to move; you don't want to get up.

It has shaken you to the core. It takes you a few moments to get yourself back to reality. As you lie there reflecting on what you just experienced, you realize that it actually occurred. That was you looking in that mirror with that aching body staring back at you…but it was a version of you in the future. You were well into your senior years in that dream; your body was aching, and you were not as mobile. You felt fragile. The dream represented you in your final days of life.

The dream has a very deep, profound impact on you. Seeing yourself in that state, and watching your life flash by like that, made you realize that your life is flashing by right now. It highlighted the areas of your life where you have been fearful, where you have not believed in yourself, and where you have prevented yourself from going the extra mile from creating the life that your heart so desired. It made you recognize how much time you have wasted carrying the burden of your past; it made you understand all the resentment and anger toward others that has been weighing you down like a ton of bricks. It made you comprehend why you have had so many blocks in your life and why things didn't work out for you. It made you realize that it was you getting in your own way and nobody else. This was contrary to what you had thought before. Often you would blame others for your situation, and when you couldn't blame another, you would blame circumstance.

Most importantly, this profound and powerful dream made you understand that all these burdens and blocks were a waste because it never had to be that way; you have the choice to live your life differently from this moment forward. After this experience, you can never take your life for granted again. The dream was the future you, years from now. Think back. As your life flashed by you when you looked into that mirror, what did it reveal?

When you are at the end of your life, what will you think looking back on your life? One day we will look in the mirror, and the image reflected back at us will not be the image that we see today. If we are fortunate to reach old age, our hair will be gray and thinned (if we are lucky to have hair at all), our hands wrinkled, our skin sagging, and maybe even our body aching.

In my experience, speaking with people who have reached their eighties, nineties, and might be lucky to be heading toward their big one hundredth, they all have seemed to say a similar thing, and that is that life goes by in a flash. And you should just relax and live your life fully and completely, while you can. Most of them tend to give similar advice, such as, "Don't worry too much what others think. Don't worry too much about the should and should nots. Don't worry so much that you never take risks because what is life without risks?"

Maybe life will not pass by as quick as it did in that dream, but the days do pass. I've noticed this myself. Many used to say to me when I was in my twenties, "Enjoy it now because it goes so quick once you hit your thirties and forties." And, in my experience, time does feel like it has sped up. Sometimes, we are conditioned to think that life gets harder or less enjoyable as we age. I refuse to believe this, so I would prefer to say, "Enjoy it now because you are alive today, and it is as great as you make it now, and always remember, this precious thing called life can keep getting better and even more fulfilling… if you allow it!" It is an attitude, a mindset. We need to flip the mindset because this thing called life, although it can be painful, scary, heartbreaking, and deeply difficult at times, is precious and amazing at the same time, but only if you chose to believe it.

Anyway, the message of this story is that life will go by. Yes, that is right – your life, my life – our lives will go by whether we like it or not. That is a fact. Now whether life goes by fast or slow is not the point. It doesn't matter. It will go by. There will be a day when each of us will look in the mirror one last time. Our life might flash by us in our mind. We don't like to think about this, but for us to live the best life today, we need to fully grasp this stark reality.

So, here is the question: When you look in the mirror that one last time, and you reflect back on the precious life that you have lived, what will your memories of your life reveal to you? Will you be proud and happy that you lived your best life? Or will it be full of regrets and wishes that you had lived it differently? Will you have taken risks and worked toward fulfilling your potential? Or will you have created a life of misery, resentment, and fear? Will you have done the things that you dreamed of doing even though you were afraid? Did you make a difference to others? Did you follow your deep passions? What is it going to be like when you look back at the end of your life?

This book has been written for the most important person on the planet. That is YOU! Although I have included stories and examples from my life, I truly hope that on some level they resonate with you at your core.

I hope that they trigger something inside you so that you choose to change your mind to work with you toward the path that will make your heart and soul sing so that at the end of your life, you can look back and say, "… (your name), gosh, I love you!!! Thank you for being brave enough to give me all those remarkable, fun, and magnificent memories. Thank you for being strong enough to be the special and authentic you. Thank you for taking risks, for getting up again when you fell so many times. Thank you for allowing me to grieve when I needed to grieve, to be angry when I felt the need to, and to show up as the magnificent, imperfect me. Thank you for the adventures, for the times that you stretched yourself and the growing and learning you were brave enough to do. Thank you for the extraordinary life that you have given me. Because of the decisions you have made in life, I have left a legacy for my loved ones and for all who have come to know me. Thank you for being courageous enough to allow me to do that. And thank you for living my life to the fullest through both the thick and thin of it!!!

In this book, we will explore the concept of your2minds, of your heart, and the truth of who you are. We will explore ideas that might stop the thought patterns and paradigms that prevent you from living the extraordinary life that you so truly deserve and that you were born to live. Before we begin, I would like to ask – are you brave enough to embark on this journey? I believe that you are. Let's do this!!

Your Extraordinary Life Exercise

"Follow your bliss and the Universe will open doors
where there were only walls."
~ Joseph Campbell

I suggest that you buy yourself a '*Your2Minds*' journal. We will be doing a number of different exercises throughout this book, which are deeply personal, and which will really help you to start changing your mind to live the best life you can. Remember, this is it. You don't get another chance to live your life, so make up your mind to live your best life now. That means doing the work, taking the time to invest in yourself, and stepping out into the fear or other emotion that may be holding you back. Make sure you do the exercises. Once you have completed this book, and the exercises in it, keep your journal because you will need to go back to it to reflect.

Before you continue reading, please take time to complete the exercise in this chapter. Although most of us don't like to think about the end of our lives, one day there will be an end. One of the most powerful things that you could do for yourself is to think about what it will be like for you at the end of your life. By accepting that we only have a limited time in this mystically beautifully precious life of ours, we will appreciate it more and be more willing to do what it takes to make it great. A lot of the spiritual teachers say that you could only live a great life by really realizing that you will be gone one day. By thinking about life from that perspective, it allows us to start appreciating every single day and every experience we have whatever that experience may be. It highlights how precious this life we have is and how much we take it for granted. Although not a philosopher but maybe a teacher, this is the one thing that Steve Jobs revealed when he discovered that he was dying.

> *"Your time is limited, so don't waste it living someone else's life. Don't be trapped by dogma – which is living with the results of other people's thinking. Don't let the noise of others' opinions drown out your own inner voice. And most important, have the courage to follow your heart and intuition."*
> ~ Steve Jobs

For this exercise, I would like you to imagine yourself looking back in that mirror ten, twenty, forty, fifty years from now. Imagine your life flashing by you. Reflecting back on what you see, I would like to go through two scenarios:

In the first scenario, imagine that your life went along the path that you are taking it currently. Be very honest with yourself. Nobody needs to know about this exercise or what you reveal in it; remember that this is about you and the most important thing to you, which is your life. Once you have that clear image of where your life would be if you continued doing what you're doing, write out the answers to the following questions:

- What types of experience, memories, situations have you accumulated?
- What regrets do you have? Out of all the regrets, which is the largest or most significant?
- What haven't you done that you would have liked to do?
- What would you have changed?
- What decisions were you afraid to make that you wished you had made?
- If you did make those decisions, what would your life have looked like; what experiences would you have had?
- What grievances and resentments did you carry?
- Would life have been more pleasant if you did not have those grievances or resentments?
- How did you contribute to others? How did you make a difference in your loved ones and other people's lives?
- Did you live your best life?

After you have honestly reflected and written those questions down, you may start the second scenario. This starts the same way; you are at the end of your life looking into the mirror, and your life flashes by you. This time, however, you have changed something in your mindset, and now you have lived the best life ever. When you have that image clearly in your mind, please answer these questions. Remember to be completely honest with yourself:

- What does it mean to have lived your best life ever? What does that look like? What does it feel like? Write an in depth description of your best life ever.
- What are some of the beautiful memories that you have?
- How do you feel when your life flashes by you?
- How did you live?
- What did you do?
- What were the things that you were afraid of, but you did not allow that fear to stop you?
- What are you most proud of?
- What made the difference to your life?
- How did you contribute to others?

You should now have a description of how you would like to live your life if you had stepped out into the fear and lived it anyway. You have a description of your great life. Now ask yourself:

- What do I need to do now, right now, to start living my best life ever?
- What do I need to change – look deep inside yourself when you're answering this question. What do I need to change within myself, within my thinking, and my behaviors, the way I treat others, the habits that I need to change?
- What do I need to do more of?
- What grievances do I need to let go of that are not serving me?
- What information do I need to make a better life for myself and my family? What course do I need to take, what book do I need to read, what research do I need to do, what professional advice or support do I need to get?
- What do I need to do to relax and have more fun?
- What do I need to do to improve my relationships with my family?
- Who do I want to be in my relationships?
- How much money do I want to earn?
- How do I want to make a real difference? What is truly meaningful to me, and how will I make this difference?

A word of warning. Some of you might be looking at your life and saying, "Well, I can't answer that question because that is not my fault. It is his fault, her fault, their fault, the boss's fault, the bank's fault, etc." I am not going to let you get away with that thinking. Nothing will change unless you take charge and become the change, implement the changes that you need to in yourself and in your life to live the life that you would truly love to live. I know that you are bigger and better than that thinking, but it is your decision to make. Nobody else can make it for you. The bottom line is that you are responsible for your life, for the decisions that you make, and for the way you use your mind to improve your life. Nobody else can make decisions for you, and nobody else can give you that extraordinary life. It is up to you.

There might be areas that you would like to change, but they won't change immediately. That is okay. When you write them down, you are imprinting them in your mind, and you are telling your subconscious mind that you would like to change that area. If you do this exercise, you will notice that you will start to get ideas about steps that you could take to make that change. Just decide to live your life the way that it will make your heart sing, and the steps you need to take will come to you. When they do come, please take the necessary steps because the only way that you will change your life from one you might regret to one that is magnificent is if you take action, even if they are small steps at first.

You might think that you already have a great life now, and that is awesome. More of us need to love our lives. I would like to challenge you to do this exercise anyway because no matter how great your life is now, there is always room for better. Why not aim for an extraordinary life? What is it in your mind that is holding you back from an extraordinary life or a life that just keeps getting better or more fulfilling?

Once you have written your answers down, reread what you have written and feel it, really feel what your life would be like if you made these changes. What does it feel like to live the life that you want to live? Take the actions that you have identified in each of those questions. What is it that you could do right now, today? Go and do it. Begin at once.

Write a list of what you could do this week, and make sure you do it. At the beginning of each week, re-examine your answers. Ask yourself if there is anything you could add. Then ask yourself, what is it that I could do today to ensure that I am living my best life, and what is it that I could do during the week? If we do not take actions every day of our precious life, that may mean we are not living our best life for that day, and what is the rest of your life? It is an accumulation of days. So, what you do today is extremely important to your life.

Keep the first script. Often with exercises like these, it is advised that you get rid of the negative or the one that you don't want, which I do agree with. For this exercise, however, I would like you to keep the first script. Then revisit that script occasionally for two reasons: First, so you can do a bit of an assessment of what other things you may be doing in your life that you missed the first time you did the exercise or that need to be improved. Second, as an important reminder, to keep you on track and also as a self-assessment on whether you are moving forward to your exceptional life or if you have slipped back into your old habits of living. If you do find yourself slipping back, that is all right as long as you re-assess and get back on track.

When you get off track, please remind yourself of the importance of your great life lived by re-reading these words from Steve Jobs:

"Remembering that I will be dead soon is the most important tool I've encountered to help me make the big choices in life.

Almost everything – all external expectations, all pride, all fear of embarrassment or failure – these things just fall away in the face of death, leaving only what is truly important.

Remembering that you are going to die is the best way I know to avoid the trap of thinking you have something to lose. You are already naked. There is no reason not to follow your heart.

No one wants to die. Even people who want to go to heaven don't want to die to get there. And yet, death is the destination we all share. No one has ever escaped it, and that is how it should be, because death is very likely the single best invention of life. It's life's change agent. It clears out the old to make way for the new."
– Steve Jobs

I Must Have Been Out of My Mind

*"When something is important enough, you do it
even if the odds are not in your favor."*
~ Elon Musk

In this chapter, and throughout this book, I will share with you some of my experiences. You may or may not relate to them, but take whatever it is that you need from them so that you may reflect on your own life, where it is currently, the emotions that you are having, and where you would like your life to go.

What could happen in only eight months is mind-boggling. Eight months ago, I left a secure job in senior management. The role, to many, appeared to be the dream role. I was working for a manager who was brilliant at what she did and was a great person too, with a great CEO, wonderful colleagues, a fabulous organization, and I had a nice salary to take home, thank you very much. I had finally started to feel comfortable. I hadn't been concerned about money for a few years; I owned two properties and was nicely building up my savings, which is not a natural thing to do for a free spirited Sagittarius.

Although I was living a nice, comfortable life, and maybe was happy to some extent, I certainly was not content. For some crazy reason, my deep core yearned for more. It was gnawing at me for quite a few years; the gnawing did not stop even with the wonderful opportunities at my amazing organization. In fact, as time went by, this gnawing became stronger.

I am an extremely sensitive "feeling" type person. I feel all emotions to their extremes, sometimes to the point of destruction. The thing with "feeling," sensitive or emotional people is that we also have very strong intuition if we allow it to come through and follow it with trust. That gut feeling that you need to do something only keeps getting stronger until you listen to it, and if you don't, it tells you that you might not only be heading down the wrong path, but you may be in trouble if you continue to travel that path. Trust me, I know, and as a result, I have learned to get my mind out of the way and listen to my gut when it speaks, even if at times, like in this situation, it seems illogical, risky, and probably not very sensible. I must have been out of my mind to leave such a great job. I am not advising you to do this. We each have to follow our own selves and our own unique path. In this situation, that gut of mine continued to tell me to take a leap of faith in myself, and in that source that lives deep within us – call it God, the Universe, spirit or whatever you may be comfortable with; to me it is all one and the same thing.

Driving in the traffic in the mornings, spending most of the day on automatic pilot and coming home to cook, clean, and go to bed, only to wake up and do it again the next day was draining the life out of me. Although I was going to a job that was great in all aspects, and I was doing my job at a high standard, I knew I was not doing my best. The passion just wasn't in me any longer, and I needed to stop for my sake, for life's sake. My loyalty led to a feeling of it not being fair for the company that I had worked for. They deserved someone who loved what they did and was able to give them their best.

The joy of living in many ways had gone. You know that feeling when you're in your twenties and thirties where you wake up, and life is exciting. I remember how passionate I used to be about work, thinking about it all the way to the office, with ideas popping up in my mind and the excitement of working with my team to implement those ideas. Without that, there was no point in continuing.

To quote Steve Jobs again: *"Your work is going to fill a large part of your life, and the only way to be truly great is to do what you believe is great work. And the only way to do great work is to love what you do. If you haven't found it yet, keep looking. Don't settle."*

Now that is a wakeup call. I was giving up my life, that joy and excitement in my life, for something that was taking up most of my time just for that pay at the end of each fortnight. Again it was not that I didn't like my job, my team. It was simply that I had lost that passion about my work, and as a result, I no longer felt that joy and sense of accomplishment.

In many ways, although I was probably meant to feel satisfied because there was no fault in any aspect of my role or work, the feeling of being trapped grew as the days went by. I felt a bit like a prisoner living in a so-called land of freedom. The best parts of my days were taken, and I had been left with a smidgen amount of time for my life, for the people I loved, and for the activities I enjoyed.

You see, I wanted to quit the job many years ago, yet that would have been ridiculous, right? I had a mortgage and had recently bought another investment property. This kept me stuck. I did not want to lose or go backward financially. I wanted to move forward. I wanted to keep moving forward, yet that intuition, that gut of mine, kept telling me to stop – my mind was telling me that I was crazy. My gut was telling me that I had no other option but stopping. For a few years prior, it had been a roller coaster of emotion while my heart battled with my mind. It was a big and crazy risk to take, yet in the end, I took that risk.

For years my heart had been yearning for more, yet for years, I did not have the courage to move on. It would be crazy, right? To add to this state, I did not know exactly what I wanted to do…at least I thought I didn't, but when I dug deeper, I did know. I had always known what I wanted to do, even as a young child. I wanted to work with people to help them find their passion and to inspire them to make it happen. My natural gift with people is to connect on a deep soul level but also to understand them and know what their own self-sabotaging behaviors may be, what their blocks are. I probably naturally knew what people's blocks are because I was "Miss Self-sabotage" myself. Throughout my life, I would often reach certain levels of success only to find myself breaking relationships, fearing people, and feeling unworthy to the point that I would ruin the success that I had managed to achieve. I had the talent, the ability, and the intelligence for great success, but my old subconscious patterns and fears would only allow me to build to a certain level before it would either have it come crumbling down or simply not allow me to go further.

Being of service to people, to inspire them to believe in themselves and to take steps toward living the life that they wanted, had been my dream for many years, for most of my life. I wanted to write, to become an author. This was a core part of my soul. I always knew that I wanted to write. Even as a child, one of my favorite things to do was to write books and to make books and illustrate them. I had so many books that I had written and illustrated, and I loved them all. I wish that I had kept some of those books, just to go back and remind myself of what I was born to do.

I did make a few attempts at writing but never completed any books. I have another two half-written books stored away on my computer. I also had a desire to work for myself. I didn't like answering to anyone, asking for permission to take a day off or to have annual leave. It is my life. Shouldn't I be the only person who permits me to live my life in any way that I choose?

It wasn't that I did not know what I wanted and what I was put on this planet to do that stopped me from stepping out and cutting ties with my so-called security. It was the flip side of my mind. Although one part of me was saying that is what I was born to do, and I knew on the deepest core level that this was right – this was my inner voice of truth – the other part of me was telling me messages from what the outside world, society, my family, and upbringing had expected. It was from this outside world I got my brutal self-punishing and detrimental voice from: that I was not good enough, that people would laugh at me, that I would lose it all, that I would be humiliated, and that I was a piece of crap. For years I had struggled on and off with depression and anxiety, and it was all because of this voice.

Please don't misunderstand my message. I do not want to put on the blame game. That is negative and a complete waste of precious time – blaming society, family, upbringing, my childhood experiences. Why would you ever want any resentment to live in and harm your body and your relationships?

I am responsible for my own life. We grow up with messages from our family, our teachers, our media, and society about the way things should be, what you should do with your life, how you should behave, what you should look like, and what your level of self-worth should be. We become conditioned to think and live in a certain way so much that we don't even realize that these were someone else's messages. We just take these messages on, and they are ingrained on a deep subconscious level in our mind. Sometimes, these messages are so deeply embedded within us that we don't stop to question them or to think about what they mean for us, whether they are right or wrong, or where they came from. We rarely reflect on how these messages affect us and our life, and we rarely challenge them to think about the possibility of whether there may be another way, whether there might be other thoughts that we could adopt. No matter where these messages came from, it is our responsibility to do so. Our own responsibility to change our mind so that we could change our life.

At times, we go through years not recognizing that we have been conditioned, and we are deeply convinced that is the way we or life is, should, or must be. We don't entertain the could or what if things turned out? or how to's. We are powerfully conditioned to keep the I should, you should, he should, she should, what if's (followed by a negative outcome), rather than asking the right questions that lead to a deeper and proper level of thought. We believe that we are thinking by going on day to day accepting our realities and that things are the way they are, and always will be the way they are, because we are living without thinking properly or deeply. Bob Proctor often states, "Two percent of people think, three percent of people think they think, and ninety-five percent of people would rather die than think."

We learn these strong beliefs about ourselves and our lives from family and school. Education is very important – I value and am deeply grateful for the education I received – but often Western education focuses on a child being obedient in class and judged by their understanding of the work that has been presented to them, or that mark that they get in an exam. The child grows up thinking that they are this mark that they received back at school. Sometimes, they may end up feeling like there is a box that they need to fit into to be accepted. No child was born to fit into a specific box. Every child is special, unique, and gifted in their way. Every child was born to contribute to the joy of this world.

Unfortunately, for some children, education does not bring out the child's talents, interests, and gifts. Every single child has their individual talents whether these are academic, creative, or different; the educational system needs to bring out these unique abilities and creativity because children were brought into this world with those gifts, and the world needs their precious contributions. No one person is better than another; we are all equally important. Can you imagine a world with an education system that captures and emphasizes the uniqueness, gifts, and talents of each child rather than just their ability to sit still, listen, and get good marks on exam papers? The world misses out by not having a system that works for all children, not just children who are able to sit still and do mathematics, reading, and writing. These subjects are important, as important as the other skills, gifts, and talents which other children have.

It is often the children that are labeled as different or that do not fit into the traditional education system that are brilliant. Nikola Tesla, one of the most powerful minds that the world has experienced, told of how he would see visions as a child. We have all heard the story of Einstein not being able to speak until he was four and unable to read until he was seven. He was deemed dyslexic and autistic. Although he excelled in mathematics, Isaac Newton did not do well in other subjects. The impact and difference that Helen Keller made on the world even though she was deaf and blind is phenomenal. The beautiful and talented Katherine Hepburn had been suspended from school due to her rebellious nature.

More recently, we have heard about one of our favorite and greatest entrepreneurs, Richard Branson, who left school as a teenager and was also dyslexic. There is also Elon Musk, who has been referred to as one of our finest and most important entrepreneurs; he was judged by doctors to have had hearing problems because of his tendency to drift off into his world and not hear those around him when he was a child. Musk was also bullied at school because he was different.

These are all examples of people who were different during the school years and who did not fit into the traditional education system yet turned out to be the genius and great talents and contributors to our world. The world would not be the same place it is today without the brilliant minds and the passionate hearts and talents of these people and so many more whom I have not listed in this book. It would be wonderful to see an educational system that accepts and embraces children who are different and works with their uniqueness so that more children could grow up knowing that they were special. This would also make them more confident as adults focusing on their dream, and as a result, our world could benefit from their unique talents and gifts.

The saddest thing is often the negative messages we receive in childhood, around not fitting into the educations system, being bullied, or being different, are often carried into adulthood preventing us from expressing our natural God-given gifts to the world. Instead, these messages continue in our mind, and sadly, we live our life using up a tiny fraction of the magnificent and infinite potential that lives within each of us.

What is Your Mind Telling You About Your Dream?

"The biggest adventure that you could ever take is to live the life of your dreams."
~ Oprah Winfrey

By the time we become adults, we often stop listening to ourselves and our hearts. Sometimes, we are so consumed by responsibility and routine that we lose that inner natural joy; we dim the natural light that we were born with. Being an ambitious dreamer, I am excited about our potential and what we could do with it. I am excited to learn about people's passions and talents and the thing that lives inside them, if they have not lost awareness of it, that excites them, that brings them joy. Throughout my life, one of my favorite questions that I have asked many people has been, "What would you do if you could do anything?" Although there have been a few people who are genuinely happy and fulfilled with where they are going, and are doing what they love for work and in life, the first thing most people say is, "Well, I would not be in this job, that's for sure!" When I press further and ask them if they are able to leave their job, and what is it that they would do if they could, they tell me their dream or, sadly, some do not even know what that dream is. Most of the time, they thought that they knew what it was they were meant to do when they were young, but with all the conditioning, messages, and paradigms that they have been living with in their mind for years, they have disconnected from the dream, or they feel confused about what it is that they really want or enjoy doing. They continue to work in their job and go day to day feeling miserable or unsatisfied, yet they accept this state because they choose to believe that there is no other way, this is all there is, and they are crazy to think that things could be different.

I never understood this type of thinking because my parents lived in poverty as children, where every day was about survival. They did not have the chance to have an education or do something better; at least that is what they thought. Although he did not have much opportunity growing up, my father had big dreams for us to do well. Because I got good grades at school, my father dreamed that one day I would become a doctor. He would always talk to me about that, and he would ask me what I wanted to be and, of course, I would answer that I would be a doctor. I never wanted to be a doctor; it did not interest me whatsoever. I wanted to work with people, to teach, to write, and to be on stage. I was born to connect with people and help them see their inner and outer beauty and potential. However, what my father did for me was extremely powerful. He taught me at a very young age to dream. He taught me that anything was possible and that there was always opportunity for me to do better and to be better, even if at times it seemed impossible.

I would dream of becoming a teacher or a performer, a gymnast, of being on stage with people watching me, or working with children and people in general, of doing humanitarian work on the other side of the world. As an adult, this deep passion for focusing on a big dream that people felt was impossible is still a deep part of me. Being a dreamer is one of the best gifts that my father gave me. It meant that I had a deep desire to be better as a person, to learn, and as a professional and to aim high in life, and expect that which I am aiming for to materialize when it is the right time. Being a dreamer has helped me understand that no matter how bad things get, things can always get better if you use your mind, your imagination. It is often the imagination that takes you to the next step, to make the impossible possible. I have witnessed this in my life repeatedly where, because of a big dream and huge imagination, I have manifested things that seemed impossible.

One of the most profound experiences where my desire was so strong that logic moved out of the way for me occurred when I was twenty-two years old. I had just completed my Bachelor of Arts Degree in psychology, and I had this humongous dream of traveling the world. For many years, my biggest desire was to do this, to go to Europe and to spend some time living and working in the United Kingdom. Now this dream was humongous because I had never been overseas alone before. I had been to Serbia twice as a child with my parents and grandmother. I had never lived on my own before either, so living in a foreign country, although I did speak the language, would have been a challenge, and I had always had my beautiful mother and father right there to support me, but in a foreign land, I would be completely on my own: nobody, not even a familiar face or a friend.

I did not have any money as I gave up my part-time job to focus on university studies during that final year. And nobody that I knew of in my Serbian community had done this. This traditional community, which I adore and feel a deep connection to, expected one to finish their studies and then think about getting married and raising a family. That was the expectation and probably the norm too. But I wasn't ready for marriage; I had a dream that I needed to realize.

I had a few close girlfriends planning a short holiday to the UK and Europe, and although I would meet them there and do some travel with them through Europe, ultimately I would take my flight out alone, traveling alone and staying there by myself for six to twelve months, not knowing anyone. Not only was I breaking the norm of my family and the community's expectation of me – the expectation of finding a man and getting married – I had completely lost my marbles and was heading out to the other side of the globe alone. What good, smart, and decent Serbian girl does that? Suzana, of course. I need to add that I was a very good, innocent, smart, and decent girl; however, I was a girl with a big dream who was not ready to give up on her dream to please anyone. It was a force that drove me, and no external influence would change that.

My parents didn't argue with me about my dream of traveling and living overseas because they probably did not believe it. It was too big of a notion to be realized and they were probably thinking, "Suzana is in la-la-land. She knows nothing about life; she will get over it."

I did my calculations, and I had six months to save $10,000, which is the amount I needed to get me overseas. I needed to find a job that paid $500 per week. Minus living expenses, I would have enough funds to get me to my dream. I did not care what I needed to do to get that $500 per week, even if it meant scrubbing toilets. I just knew I had to get it. Now, $500 per week in Australia back in 1995 was a pretty decent salary, so I was unlikely to get that salary cleaning, but my dream and the naivety of my youth knew that I would get it. I remember standing in the kitchen while my mum had been mopping the floor telling her how much money I needed to get me overseas and that I was looking to become a cleaner to earn my $500 per week. My mother laughed out loud. "As if you will ever get anywhere near $500 per week cleaning! Are you mad!" I simply replied, "Watch me!" and the conversation was over.

I spent the rest of the day working on my resume and thought about where I could go to personally distribute my resume and ask for work. There was an industrial area about four kilometers from where we lived, and they had recently built warehouses there for the local shopping centers. I decided that I would go to each of those warehouses and give each of them a copy of my resume. I parked my car outside the first warehouse, got out, and nervously started to walk toward the front door. It was quite a distance between the car park and front door, probably at least one hundred and fifty meters, in my mind anyway. As I walked, I remember my nerves building up. I desperately needed a job, but I was a very shy and insecure young person especially when I had to speak with someone older or who had a bit of authority. I saw two men standing in suits smoking in front of the building right next to the front door. One noticed me approaching first, and he said, "And who are you?" I cannot remember what I said. It was all a blur. My nerves had taken over me, but I managed to tell him that I was looking for work, I didn't care what that work was, and I would be happy to clean toilets, as I handed him my resume. He replied, "Sure, I will give it to our Operations Manager." I thanked him and left.

When I got back to my car, I sat there for a few minutes, my body shaking. I planned to submit my resume to each of the warehouses on that street. I knew I had to do this to increase my chances of getting that job. I walked to the next place but couldn't get in as there were boom gates. I did not dare to go up to security and give them my resume, so I headed back to the car and sat there trying to contain my nerves, but they wouldn't settle so, disappointed in myself, I drove back home.

I was working at a nearby petrol station. It wasn't a terrific job, and I was making barely enough money to pay for my small living expenses let alone to save for an overseas trip. I got nervous because I felt the days were passing, and I had not yet secured the job I needed to achieve my dream. I was getting ready for work one day, about a week after I had submitted my resume to that man who was smoking in front of the warehouse when the phone rang. I picked up the phone, and it was a man asking to speak with me. "Hello, Suzana, this is so and so from the distribution center. Mr. Jude has given me your resume. We have a job opening as an accounts manager in our office. Would this be something that you would be interested in?"

My thoughts during this conversation: "What? An accounts manager? He is talking to me about an office job? Even though I have no experience. Really? Wow!" I never thought anyone in the world would hire me for a job like that, so I didn't even think of applying for that kind of work! We arranged a time to meet, which I thought was to be an interview.

When I arrived at the distribution center, I was walking through the car park about to enter the yard, and I noticed a boom gate, as I tried to walk through, a man in a uniform stopped me asking me who I was and what I was doing there. He was the security guard. When I explained that I was meeting with the Operations Manager, he made me sign in. He called the manager on the phone, and only then did he allow me to walk through to the office. Funnily enough, I did not even notice the boom gate last time I was there when I submitted my resume to that man at the front door.

I met with the Operations Manager, and it felt more like a discussion rather than an interview. I had been anxious and shy, so I felt as though I hadn't performed well enough to get the job. As I was walking out of the Operations Manager's office, I bumped into the same man I had given my resume to. I had discovered that he had been the CEO. By chance, luck, or my own will manifesting this, the day that I submitted my resume, I bypassed the guard and went straight to the CEO without even knowing there should have been a guard there or that he was the CEO! Anyway, I ended up getting the job, and it paid me $530 per week, thank you very much. I think that is when my mother learned never to judge or challenge my determination. It wasn't until after I started the role that I discovered by company policy, the security guard was never to leave the security booth. There always had to be someone in that booth; I think from memory that there were two security guards working in the booth. It was his job to have constant surveillance of the premises and not to allow unauthorized persons into the premise. Well, that responsibility had been thrown out the door by a young lady who had been compelled to realize her dream.

I remember sitting on that plane excited but so fearful and extremely nervous as I had never done anything this big alone. I had not even been to another state in Australia alone, and here I was going halfway around the world all on my own and without Mum and Dad to save me if I ever needed their support or help.

Of course, I had a marvelous time traveling, living, and working in the UK. I have stories and wonderful memories that I will cherish for the rest of my life. But apart from the fantastic experiences that I had on this incredible adventure, I gained so much more deep inside me. *I learned with a decision, determination, belief, and action, the rational and logical moves out of the way while the Universe steps in to help you get to where you are heading.* I now have a deep knowing of this, and I came back with the knowing that I can achieve anything, if I really, really want it. That was the biggest lesson I learned, which has guided me thereafter. I had experienced the magic for the first time, and I knew that I could experience it over and over again. Beyond that I came home a different person; I developed an understanding of who I was at the deep core level. I developed an understanding of life in a way that I could not explain in words, and most importantly, my belief in the unknown, in source, spirit, or God was unbreakable. And from that one experience, I inspired others to step out in determination to do what it is that they really wanted. I learned a deep dream, a determined mind, and the courage to act allows the Universe to come and prepare the way for you.

I could never understand people who just accepted their miserable reality convincing themselves that this is all there is, and things just cannot and will not get better. "That's life," you would hear them say. Oh dear, really?? Seriously? This *is* life, and it is the most amazing, glorious, magical thing that you will experience.

That is not to minimize or ignore the situation of some people who are going through terrible experiences, such as losing a child or loved one, violence, or mental illness . I would never undermine these difficulties. We are alive as human beings to experience both, to experience the full pallet, the full colors of life, and being alive means allowing yourself to feel all emotions. Contrast is a Universal law. We all have our dark nights of the soul, and this is a natural part of life. We just need to allow ourselves to go through them, to feel the emotions as they come up, and to tread lightly and gently. Being gentle on ourselves during these times is critical, but we must be diligent about what thoughts are coming up for us. We must ensure that they are not thoughts that tell ourselves: "I should be…"; "I should have"; "You idiot"; or any other of the sort. These thoughts are unnecessary, untrue, and often dig the hole deeper. Without experiencing the dark, we might not appreciate the light. These times often make us assess our situations, and often through them a birth of a new idea, a new way of being, a new mission or purpose is born. They allow us to assess and then conceive a new desire, a new life, a new reality for ourselves and maybe even for others.

It is when people feel stuck, and allow themselves to believe that there is no other way, that they have to stay miserable because they have to continue to pay the bills, so there is no point in wanting more or entertaining the idea about the possibility of another way. This is particularly sad. Being a dreamer and dreaming about "the way out there" helped me get through some of my lower points or through tasks that I did not enjoy because it left me with the hope of something more, the excitement about something bigger and better, even when the dream had felt at the time to be too big ever to be realized. Our mind is the most powerful resource and gift, we can use it to propel us forward or we keep us stuck for a longer period than necessary.

There are also the people who know what they want and would love to step out and do something different; they have dreams about their lives whether they be about their dream work, relationships, or life in general. Sometimes though, when you ask people why they aren't doing what they would like to do, the answer illustrates that their deep subconscious paradigms have kicked in. When you dig deeper, you realize that all their excuses are associated with deep fear – the fear of not being good enough, the fear of losing everything and ending up on the streets, the fear of being hurt, the fear of rejection. In today's world, this fear is amplified by the constant messages portrayed in the media and the world around us. Most of us have been brutal toward ourselves. Most of us would be appalled if our partner or boss or a stranger talked to us the way we talk to ourselves.

Please know that I am not advising you or anyone to quit work and go for your dreams. That is not what I am saying. For me quitting work was the only option at the time because that inner knowing inside me continued to get louder. I know that it was not a logical or rational decision, but I also knew that whatever happened, I would be all right. Over the years, I have developed that inner knowing and self-trust. I am not suggesting that you do the same. You have your intuition and inner guidance, and you know what is right for you. What I am saying and what I would like to gently and loving nudge you to do is to decide what it is that you want and what would truly and deeply make you happy, and step out and start working on that thing that you believe would really make your heart sing.

You could start working on your dream while you hold on to your job; you could put aside an hour a day to simply start it. If it is a new career, explore it, do that course, start to develop that website. If it is love or a dream relationship, start understanding yourself first and why you are attracting what you are now. Start to change what you need to inside yourself, and then step out and have that one date. If it is writing that book, get up an hour early, or take that week's long vacation as I did and just start writing. These small steps are ways that you could work toward your dream gently. Putting the small steps in place might make it easier for you to start taking some bigger steps toward your dream and living your best life. Remember to notice your mind and when it may be giving you a false and destructive message. Notice it and flip it over, baby!! You are a rock star!! You can do this!!!

And then there are those who take life by its horns and say, "#!@* it! We only live this life once. Let's just live it!!" They are the risk takers, the doers, the people who have the fear but step out into that fear and make it happen. I love these people. They inspire the socks off me. They remind me not to settle and get too comfortable because you truly feel alive when you are stepping out of your comfort zone, taking steps toward that desire or dream. They remind me when I start to settle in my own misery to snap out of it and focus on what I want and where I want to go, be, have, or experience in life. They remind me that training my mind to focus on where I do want to go will bring me so much more than allowing my mind to focus on the aspects that I do not like about myself, life, others or my fears.

These people make the impossible possible. They are the business women who are also mothers, they are the mountain climbers, the people who may have experienced a terrible accident and life changes, and they end up running marathons. They are the people who are naturally shy and insecure but end up being fabulous public speakers. They are the parents who are pushing their boundaries to become better, to live better. They are the doctors, the teachers, who decide one day that they want something more, so they embark on an adventure to travel or start a charity. They are the warehouse workers who decide they deserve something bigger, so they go out and get that degree or they open up that animal shelter that they have dreamed about doing. They are the ones who fail many times, have many challenges, yet get back up again, ready to give it another go, ready to put their boxing gloves on and go for another round.

This inspiring person is in all of us. It just takes courage and the willingness to take the first step and not let your thoughts get in the way when the going gets tough. Remember, you are never a failure if you step out of your comfort zone to manifest a dream and you keep trying. Hillary failed twice before he made it to the summit of Mount Everest. We all have a Hillary inside us when we develop our will, imagination, desire, and belief to be strong enough, when we use our mind to work for us and not against us.

If you feel that you have a deep desire or dream for something different and something more, I cannot stress enough how important it is to get a coach and an accountability partner. A coach will believe in you and keep your vision, particularly when your paradigms start to kick in and when you feel like you want to quit. Every successful person I know has had a coach or a mentor. When I was working in senior management, I always had a supervisor whose function was very similar to that of a coach. I was accountable to this person, and this person held a vision of where I needed to go even during the times that it got tough for me and when I could not see what the next step was.

Your dream is extremely important to you and your life. I know beyond a shadow of a doubt that you can achieve that one thing that you would like to achieve or do. I don't care what your story is, but it is so easy to quit. It is so easy to allow our paradigms to continue to control us even though they are self-sabotaging. If you quit and give up on your dream, you live your life thinking, "I should have", "why didn't I?", "I could have" instead of looking back at your life with a sense of pride, accomplishment, or at the very least, the courage to have given it your best shot.

We humans are interesting creatures. As brilliant, amazing, wonderful, genius, and remarkable each of us are, we are often a juxtaposition – we carry the opposite and can be mean, self-sabotaging, fearful, and, unfortunately, violent to ourselves and others. But this is a choice – you can follow your brilliance, your intuition, your positive self-talk, or you can follow the destructive and negative patterns. You make the choice about how to use your mind.

Sometimes it can be a challenge to flip the side of your mind into your brilliance, your beauty, and what is great about yourself and this moment. At times we tend to focus on the outside world or our previous experience of being in a dysfunctional family, trauma, and the world around us, which is often designed to illicit fear, distrust, and feelings of inadequacy. This is especially true if you follow media or the advertising that we are swarmed by in our society today. This type of thinking, however, does not serve us in any way, shape, or form.

If I could say only one thing that I know for sure, that would be that each of us was born pure, beautiful, and perfect. Unfortunately, due to our external influences and our deep paradigms, we forget this somewhere along the way. That is the saddest thing because even as adults, each of us still has incredible beauty, light, and genius within us, no matter where you are at or what your circumstances are in life. The problem is our minds are so full of harsh self-criticism, fear, and conditioning that we often cannot see past this. We all have a guidance system within us, the voice of God, our intuition that never leaves us, if we are willing to allow it to speak, if we are willing to allow ourselves to be still and quiet for long enough to hear that nudging internal voice. And once we hear that voice, if we are brave enough to step out and follow the direction in which we are guided, even if we feel fear, we begin to experience things that we may have never imagined. We all have a deeply connected, deeply knowing voice; this voice is the voice of our spirit, of our source, of God. Ultimately, it is a choice. We can listen to the negative, self-destructive mind or the deeply connected, deeply knowing mind.

How do we connect and hear this voice within us? Different people do this in different ways. I learned to strengthen my inner voice by putting my focus and attention on it. I have learned to trust it, and the more I prove that I trust it by taking actions according to its direction, the stronger it has become and the more it serves me as a result.

Sometimes, if I am not clear about the message or the direction, I invite my inner voice or intuition to speak to me. I often notice it through feeling. The feeling in my stomach is how I hear it most often. I ask it questions, and I listen for the answer, which often comes with a feeling from deep within my core. At times, I feel the presence around me. Many times when I have felt worried, I opened up to it and felt its guidance and protection. I had to practice tapping into my inner voice or intuition, particularly when I have gone through difficult times because that is when my mind is clouded, and I have allowed the negative self chatter to take over my own deep, inner knowing. When I allowed that chatter to become stronger, I noticed that the chatter overrides that beautiful guiding voice of my soul, so it makes it more challenging to hear its message. During these times, it is extremely important for me to be still and quiet and get into my daily practice of prayer and meditation. It is critical for me to connect with source, with God, or my inner knowing, so I have to quiet down my critical mind and allow my connection and trust to enter and to take over again.

What Would You Do if It Was Guaranteed That You Couldn't Fail?

This exercise has been designed to make you start dreaming, to begin connecting to your inner source, your deep guidance, and your intuition. It is a way to allow your ideas and creativity and heart to flow without the criticism and fear of your mind. If your mind tries to take over during this exercise with its chatter and negativity, which it will probably try to do, let the chatter run freely without getting caught up in it, without letting it take over. It is normal to have some of this chatter as that is the function of the brain. Just don't buy into it. I thank that thought and then imagine wrapping it up with love. What works for me while I do this, and I would invite you to try this, is to listen to music that I love, that speaks to my heart, meditation or relaxing music without too many words for this exercise. I also light a candle. I love candles; they create ambiance and illicit a relaxed feel.

Make sure you are in a place where you will not be interrupted. Take a few moments to relax. Relax your body. Start from your toes and feel and relax your muscles working your way through your body to your head. Go back, and relax the beautiful organs within your body. Now relax your mind. Tell it there is nothing to worry about. There is nothing that needs to be done right now. You are completely safe. This is your time, and you have the right to feel nice and relaxed.

Once you are relaxed, connect with your heart. Tell your heart how much you appreciate everything it does for you. Your heart continues to pump blood throughout your body and keeps you alive. Your heart allows you to experience beautiful emotions and the beauty of another person, of music, art, and other areas and situations that make a difference in your life.

Once you have thanked your heart, and you feel connected to it, lovingly tell your heart that it is its turn to talk to you. Tell it that, although for many years you have not known to connect to it and hear its gentle whispers of love, you are now ready. Tell it that you are ready to hear its messages and its guidance. Take a few moments to do this.

When you feel that you are connected with your heart, ask your heart the following questions:

- If I could do anything without fail, what would I do? What is that thing that would make my heart sing?
- What is the thing that I was born to do?
- How can I serve you, my heart?
- What is one step that I could take toward this?

Have Your2Minds journal near you while you are doing this exercise. Write down whatever comes to you from your heart regarding these questions. Watch your mind when you do this exercise. What is it saying to you? Write this down in Your2Minds journal too.

Once you have completed this exercise, look at the thoughts you've written down in Your2Minds journal. Ask yourself:

- How do I change them?
- What is stopping me from taking that first step?
- What could I do today to take that first step? Write it down, and set some time aside to do it. The first step does not have to be a big one; a small, easier step is better than not taking any action at all.

Watching your mind, and writing your thoughts down in Your2Minds journal is important because it allows you to connect, identify, and recognize what you need to do. By identifying them, you can work on changing them.

Practice this exercise as often as you can. Sometimes, the answers may not be clear the first few times you do this exercise. This may be because you are not used to doing this. You may not be accustomed to connecting to your heart. You may even have been living your life through the fear driven chatter of your mind. That is okay if you have. Practice this exercise, and practice listening to your heart's message to yourself. The more you practice, the stronger your messages will become. By a message, I mean a thought or, predominantly, a feeling. Your feelings will tell you if it is the right thing for you. You may feel excited by the message, and you might even feel the excitement mixed with some fear. This shows that you are on track because the message you're receiving to do the thing that excites you is probably a big thing that you may not have ever achieved before. It is natural to feel fear when we are embarking on new grounds.

Your2Minds

"The human mind is constantly attracting vibrations which harmonize with that which dominates the mind. Any thought, idea, plan, or purpose which one holds in one's mind attracts a host of its relatives, adds these 'relatives' to its own force and grows until it becomes the dominating motivating master of the individual in whose mind it has been housed."
~ Napoleon Hill

May 2017, the decision was made, and I hadn't been working as a full-time employee for over three months. Although I had a period of winding down and enjoyed "my time" to wake up whenever I wanted, walk on the beach, and go to the local cafe and just read, I had never been without work, so the reality of not having a fortnightly pay come in started to really kick in. I wanted to work in my own business, a business in which I could inspire and work with people so that they could realize their potential, and I wanted to write. So, I decided to become a Proctor Gallagher Institute (PGI) Consultant. Becoming a PGI Consultant was exciting for me because it would train me to deliver Bob Proctor's twelve lesson program and assist people to refine their goals and finally transform their self-sabotaging paradigms to more constructive paradigms that would allow them to have the success in life that they had always dreamed of having. This was perfect because it was what I always wanted to do, work with people so that they could see their own uniqueness and personal power and break through the boundaries that blocked them from being who they had dreamed of becoming, living and achieving their most wonderful life. This had always been my passion and one of the reasons why I chose to study psychology at university. I was interested in people, in human behavior, and in helping people break through their own negative patterns.

Initially, I was so excited. Unexpectedly, shortly after my enrollment to become a Proctor Gallagher Consultant, my own very deeply embedded paradigms started to kick in. I was overwhelmed with anxiety, fear, and shame. "What if I fail at this, what will people think?", "But I have tried to do things before, and they haven't worked." "What if I go back to full-time work again? That would mean I am a failure. That is very shameful!" "Everyone will be talking about me. Everyone will think I am a failure!" and the brutally destructive thoughts started to kick in. At the same time, I had no income come, so can you imagine my thoughts and panic around that?? I continued digging my hole with my thoughts; I woke up around four o'clock every morning overwhelmed with so much anxiety that there were nights where I was honestly praying that I would get through the night without dying. The pain I felt was deep; some mornings it almost felt like physical pain. It was truly like a nightmare, yet I was awake.

My vibration at this stage must have been so negative that it was affecting all aspects of my life including my relationship. On some level, I was pushing my partner away too. To top it off, I had a miscarriage the previous year. Although I have always wanted to be a mother, that was the first time I had been pregnant; had I not had the miscarriage, the baby would have been due in June right smack bang in the middle of this terrible time. The day the baby was due, I wanted to be completely alone. I felt I did not grieve properly when I had the miscarriage. I wanted this day to myself. It was the worst period that I have gone through in years, and I needed some space. Ironically, and like God or the Universe had something against me, I went for a walk down the street to my local cafe, and out of everyone I could have bumped into, I had to bump into a dear friend who had given birth to her baby son only three weeks ago. Boy, was that a jab in the heart – another one.

A few months prior to this event, I had it all, and now it felt like everything I had was being pulled from under my feet. I was losing all hopes, all dreams, and all my confidence. I was stuck in such a dark place, I felt that I would never get out of it. I feel very vulnerable sharing this with you, but it is through our courage to tell the tale that we connect and see our strength. I will also tell you that there were some days that I wished I could just go, take my life there and then. Fortunately, and with the help of some amazing and wonderful people, I kept putting one foot in front of the other, one very small step at a time. Looking back, I know the reason why I went so far into a dark hole: deep down, I felt deeply unworthy. I was afraid, and I did not believe that I could be a success in business or life. On some profound level, I was more concerned about what the world would think about me rather than what I truly wanted. I had let the thoughts and feelings of unworthiness take control of me before I took control of them.

Through this dark period, I discovered the concept of Your2Minds. Well, it wasn't really a discovery; it came to me. I had been looking for a business name for a few months, and all the names that came to mind, for one reason or another, did not feel right. One day while lying on a massage table at the local massage place in the beach side suburb of St Kilda, Melbourne, I finally allowed a bit of relaxation to enter my body. While I was being massaged, the name Your2Minds flowed into my mind. I remember walking out, feeling, "Yep, this is it. I've got it!' The first time in all those dreaded months I felt a sense of excitement.

So, why Your2Minds? What is the significance? What did Your2Minds mean to me? Why was I excited? Your2Minds had enormous significance to me, and that is why it resonated so deeply within me. It signifies:

- our own two minds: the conscious and subconscious minds.
- the two voices in our head: one voice telling you that you are great, you can do this, and the other voice telling you that you are unworthy and cannot do anything right.
- being in 2Minds: when you are unsure about something and you are finding it difficult to make a decision.
- the power of 2Minds working together to create something significantly bigger and better. Two people fully focused and in harmony on pushing each other forward into greater and bigger realms or two people fully focused and working in harmony to create a significant idea or project.

I had used all three of these areas previously, and I knew that I could also use these to get me out of the terrible rut that I had been in. Sharing this part of my experience feels vulnerable, but when you are in such a dark place, sometimes getting up in the morning is difficult. I knew, however, that to change anything, I must have daily discipline. I did this by practicing the exercises that I had in my Proctor Gallagher Institute's Thinking Into

Results program. The work from Thinking Into Results is extraordinary – the program works on changing the beliefs that are deeply embedded in your mind that do not serve you. By permanently changing these beliefs, or paradigms, you will see a change in your attitude, behavior, and, ultimately, your results. Life just works when you know how to use your mind. You can create changes in any and all of the areas in your life by learning how to retrain or reprogram your mind.

It was not until I had explored some of the concepts in *A Course in Miracles* that I recognized that I had completely lost trust – trust in myself, trust in life, and trust in God. I realized that nothing would change until I developed trust and belief again. I also grasped that although I was applying the work from the Thinking Into Results program, it was more like ticking boxes, and I was not taking it to the deeper level that the program requires you to do. The voices in my head were continuously telling me that I was not good enough, that I would fail, and be put to shame. "What will people think of me?" was a common one, and, of course, that I was not worthy of the success that I had dreamed of having. So, I had to push that discipline further. I had to really connect to that inner core of me, my spirit again, and I did this by:

- continuing my Thinking Into Results lesson every day.
- practicing "Let Go and Let God!" I would say this affirmation over and over again, and I would envision all my inner organs that were holding strongly onto fear letting go and relaxing.
- mirror work, affirmations, story scripts, and affirmations at night.
- daily meditation and weekly meditation classes.
- prayer with a partner (it's amazing what one prayer with two people intent on resolving my issue did).
- sharing this situation with my beautiful and incredible meditation teacher. She would connect with me regularly, encourage me forward, focus on my getting out of the rut. Looking back now, I can see that she was playing the role of my accountability partner.
- Having daily support from my amazing best friend, whom I trust and who has always been there for me through thick and thin.

This all might sound like a lot of work, but when you are in such a state, you need to have the mindset that you will do whatever it takes to get out of that rut. It is like any principle of success; it takes commitment, action, and the attitude of doing whatever it takes. Of course, as it usually is, the work was worth it in the end. Shortly after combining all this, I noticed something had lifted, and a week or two later, I was approached to do some consulting work. I had funds to go to Toronto to do my training with Bob Proctor, and my relationship with my partner improved dramatically. It all happened at once, but I had to change my mind, change my old paradigms that were not serving me, before I could experience the change. I had to lift my vibration to what I wanted and not what I did not want. I had to become the person that I wanted to be in my mind first. I had to do this with trust and belief that everything was going to fall into place, and it did. It is absolutely phenomenal that when you do the work, work on your subconscious paradigms, on your precious and brilliant mind by changing your mindset and lifting your vibration, the things you have wanted just flow to you easily and naturally.

Your2Minds Exercise

*"If you want to find the secret of the universe,
think in terms of energy, frequency and vibration."*
~ Nikola Tesla

This book will go into each of the above areas and guide you through some powerful exercises to help move you forward in any area that you would like to apply them to. Each section has a broader dedication to these areas. For now, please think of an area in your life that you may find a little challenging or that you would like to work on to get exceptional results. Please work through and write your answers to the following questions in your Your2Minds journal.

- What is the area that you would like to focus on?
- What has happened in this area when you have tried to get better results previously? Explain what happens
- What results are you getting in that area?

- Is there a pattern? Do you get similar results?
- If you are getting similar results, what do you think is the message or paradigm that your subconscious mind is holding on to? (It is usually the result that you get over and over again.)
- What vibration do you think you send out unconsciously?
- Be very clear about your mind. What messages come up for you in regards to this situation? Are they positive or negative?
- How could you change these to messages that are more loving to you and that would serve you?
- Are you in 2Minds about this situation?
- Whom could you trust and work with as an accountability partner?
- Is there anyone that you would be able to work with on a spiritual level?

Answering these questions honestly is important. We can only change ourselves and, therefore, the results that we are experiencing in our lives by first understanding who we are and where we currently are in our thinking. After you have answered the questions, and written down your honest answer to each, I would like you to write a detailed answer to the following questions. The more detail you go into, the better this exercise works because you are painting a picture in your mind of what you would like it to be like, and with repetition, you will impress your subconscious mind:

- If anything were possible, and you knew you would not fail, what results would you like to get?
- What pattern or habits do you need to develop to make this new way of being or these exciting new results a reality?
- What is the new message that you would like to develop in your mind, a positive message that will assist you in moving forward toward the results that you want?
- What are the feelings associated with these new results? How do you feel when you imagine yourself having these new results or imagine this new way of being? Your emotions are very important because the emotions will lift your vibration, and your vibration will get you moving toward your new goal. The Universe will respond to your new vibration by moving the new result or new way of being closer to you when you start to step out into action. It is the way that the Law of Vibration, which is a primary law, and the Law of Attraction work.

- What will the new message from your mind be?
- If you are in 2Minds about a situation, make sure you take some time to clear that confusion up. Decide what it is you want and stick to it. You need to have a clear mind so that the Universe may respond. Otherwise you will be sending out a vibration of confusion and a lack of clarity, which will bring a frantic state to your results.
- If you have an accountability partner, get working with them, and check in with them on a daily basis ("The Power of Two Minds Working Together in a Spirit of Harmony" chapter has a great method that you can implement with your accountability partner). If you cannot find an accountability partner at this stage, that is okay too. Just keep doing the work. Become self-disciplined, and do these exercises with yourself for the benefit of yourself.

The Conscious and Subconscious Minds

*"Self-sabotage is like a game of mental tug-of-war.
It is the conscious mind versus the subconscious mind where
the subconscious mind always eventually wins."*
~ Bo Bennett, American Businesswoman

Our conscious and subconscious minds have been studied by psychologists and philosophers for centuries. Freud probably popularized the subconscious mind in the modern world. He spoke about the different layers of the mind, where approximately ten percent of our thoughts are conscious thoughts, and the remainder reside in the subconscious and unconscious minds. This is astounding. Although we think that we are deep thinking beings, most of our thinking, emotions, behaviors, and results are below the levels of conscious thoughts.

To keep it simple, our minds function on two levels. One is the surface level, the level from which our thoughts stem; this is the conscious. The other deeper level is the emotional level; it is our subconscious. Often we are not aware of the subconscious mind, yet it controls a significantly large, some say as much as ninety-five to ninety-eight percent, of all our behavior and the results that you continue to get in all areas of your life.

The subconscious mind absorbs everything that we see, feel, and experience: everything. It is nondiscriminatory and will absorb all the information around it or that you experience. The information you hear, the sights you are seeing, the thoughts that you are thinking, the emotions that you are feeling, the experiences that you are having are all automatically captured by the subconscious mind. Luckily, your conscious mind, which is referred to as the thinking mind, can be used as a filter of what reaches your subconscious mind. By not allowing any emotion to be attached to the thing that we are experiencing, it is less likely to have an impact on our subconscious mind, often referred to as the feeling mind. In other words, the subconscious mind can be impressed in two ways: through repetition, which is sped up if backed up by emotion or a strong emotional impact. In this way, we have control by what we allow to enter our subconscious mind.

This is why when we have experienced a deep traumatic event, behavior often changes automatically. An incident that is traumatic produces shock to the brain, and there is an immediate impact to the subconscious. Not only the traumatic events change the subconscious mind, but also positive events have the same level of impact. This is both an unfortunate as well as fortunate matter. It is unfortunate because in life, more often than not the incident is a negative or traumatic experience that has had the impact. The fortunate part is that if we know that a strong positive emotional impact can affect the subconscious mind, we can develop strong positive emotion to influence and diminish the negative impact imprinted on the subconscious.

We can see the power of our subconscious mind in our lives. Think of a time where you experienced a shocking situation. It could have been the experience of being bullied at school or a car accident, or you may have been bitten by a dog. If you can remember the whole incident, you probably did not have the same particular reaction to that thing – whether it be anxiety when you are in a social setting, getting behind the wheel of a car, or when a dog approaches – before the incident occurred compared to after the incident. This is your subconscious reacting to that particular object. That shock that you had during the incident, that intense emotion of fear and feeling overwhelmed was imprinted on your mind, and now whenever you are put in a situation in which that object representing the cause of the shock or threat appears, your subconscious mind will react, and your conscious mind will think quickly to keep you safe and away from the threat.

The biggest change in my behavior that I can remember due to an incident in adulthood occurred when I was in London. I became a live-in carer for the elderly during my post university adventure in the UK. I was living and caring for a marvelous and fascinating woman who was ninety-six years of age. Agatha had been the child of an extremely wealthy

Estonian family that had migrated to the UK when she was just a child. She was the only child and inherited the entirety of her family's wealth. Agatha was fortunate to enjoy this great wealth. When she was younger, she had her own chauffeur and was whisked around in prestigious cars. Agatha must have been one of the most interesting people I ever met. The stories she shared with me were so different from what I had experienced growing up in the working class suburb of Campbellfield, on the outskirts of Melbourne. Our worlds regarding upbringing, life experience, and social status had been miles apart, yet we managed to develop a nice bond and friendship in the short time that we had known each other.

Agatha's townhouse in South Kensington, London, was four stories tall and full of immaculate decoration. I couldn't believe my eyes when Agatha showed me her entertainment room; it was filled with exquisite artwork that had all been authentic. Some appeared to be authentic Renaissance pieces. I could have sworn that I had studied some of her authentic paintings during my art class at secondary school. My favorite, the four exquisite paintings of a beautiful Goddess, each representing a season.

The evenings at Agatha's place were usually non-eventful and quiet. We talked about the good old days. As she shared wonderful stories of her interesting life, she would do a card reading for me. Agatha was quite psychic and did readings using a normal deck of cards. At times we would watch television, and Agatha would be in bed by nine-thirty at the latest.

One particular day, I woke up with a terrible feeling in my gut. Something was not right, and I just did not want to be there. That was strange because, after a tough period of getting settled so far away from home, I usually enjoyed my days in London with Agatha. I could not explain the feeling I had that morning, but I wanted to jump out of my skin. Something was about to happen, but I did not know what. I desperately wanted to get on a plane and fly all the way back home to Australia. I got down on my knees and prayed. I prayed with all the intensity that I could muster. Something was happening. I needed to get out of the house. I needed to go, but I did not know where. The day went by. Nothing happened, but that feeling of overwhelming discomfort stayed with me. The evening drew near, and Agatha and I sat in her lounge room watching the three tenors. It was a lovely concert to watch, this elegant performance of true genius. Agatha stayed up past her bedtime. She was tapping her finger on her chair, and although she was clearly enjoying herself, I remember thinking how odd it was that she stayed up so late. She would be in bed by nine o'clock every evening aside from the occasional nine-thirty late night. It was strange. Thinking back now, I wonder if Agatha also shared the same terrible gut feeling that I had that day.

At exactly six minutes past ten, the doorbell rang. That was really strange because nobody visited us past seven o'clock in the evening. By this stage, my gut was screaming at me not to open that door. As I walked to the front door, my gut was telling me to go back and ask who it is. The flip side of my mind, the side that gets one into trouble, told me not to ask who it was because it was probably just my boyfriend or one of Agatha's friends. It would have been embarrassing to ask who it was if it was them. In reality, I don't know why asking who it was would have been embarrassing. I feel a little embarrassed at even having had that thought in retrospect. That was such an irrational thought, but that was what the negative side of the mind told me, and mistakenly, I chose to listen to it and go against my gut.

To this day, over twenty years after the event, I remember every thought that went through my mind during that short walk, that seemed like a long walk, to the front door. Deep inside me, I knew what was about to take place was going to change my life forever, and I knew it was not going to be a pleasant experience. Even by knowing that, however, for whatever reason, I chose to listen to the mind, which convinced me not to be stupid by asking who was at the other side of the door ringing that doorbell. As a result of this decision, I ended up opening the door to three men wearing balaclava. The shock I felt was beyond comprehension. I screamed with terror. I was petrified. In my mind, I was going to die, and there was no doubt about it. That was it for me. The interesting thing was, when I look back now, I was not afraid of dying at all. The fear I felt was more for my parents who would have had to experience the loss of a child on the other side of the world. I had to push past them and get onto High Street, which was a couple of houses down. High Street was always busy, and that way we would be safe.

Unfortunately, even with all that adrenaline pumping through my body, I did not manage to muster enough strength to push my way through the three men onto the road. The men pushed past me and entered the house. One told me not to fight them and we would be safe. He took me to the room where Agatha sat and asked Agatha for her jewelry. Agatha remained extremely calm – it was just a man wearing a balaclava over his face standing in her lounge room – and told him that she didn't have any jewelry. Yeah, right, she didn't have any jewelry! One of her paintings would have set you up for life. It was obvious she had a lot of jewelry, but for whatever reason, the man did not question it and left the room. I tried to cover the two silver rings that I had recently bought in Florence, Italy. They would hardly set you up for your life: maybe a week if you were really tight with your spending. Nevertheless, they were precious to me, so I hid my hands under my thighs.

The break-in, luckily, only lasted a few minutes. When the man left the lounge room, Agatha grabbed the key and locked us both in the room. We got on the phone and called the police. I was so petrified that I could not even string a sentence together. The police arrived within minutes, and they did a search throughout the house. We were told that the men had run straight up to the top floor. There was a couple who had lived on the top floor, and as they tried to break into their room, the man who lived there had thrown a kettle at them, so they all ran out. It turned out that the man had been a jewelry shop owner, and he was going to fly out to Dublin that evening to spend Christmas with his wife's family. Fortunately for us, that afternoon they had decided not to take that flight.

Ever since that incident, I do not like being alone in large houses. I do not like the sound of doorbells either, particularly at night. To this very day, when I do find myself in a large home alone, I have to be very aware of my thoughts and tell myself to calm down and that I will be safe. Otherwise I would be shaking with fear just by being alone in the house.

Recently, I decided to go and stay at my parent's place because they were overseas on vacation. Their house is not huge, but it sure is big enough to elicit this fear in me. My partner decided to surprise me by popping by after he had finished work. It was late at night, and I was on the phone with a friend trying to work out my website. The first time he knocked, I heard it, but I ignored it because my immediate reaction was terror and, automatically, my body shook. My immediate reaction took me to three men waiting outside ready to attack me. I ignored the knock hoping whoever was there would go away. Just that one knock, and my body immediately reacted. I didn't want to face it, so I continued to ignore it. My partner knocked on the door again, and automatically, my body went into a frenzy of fear. It was trembling, and he hadn't even rang the doorbell yet. My mind went straight to a stranger trying to break in to kill me. I mean, who else would be knocking on the door at nighttime? My body was shaking. I was petrified. I couldn't ignore the door this time because whoever was out there had continued to knock. If I didn't answer, maybe they would break in and then I would be in trouble, so my mind thought. I would have to relive the terrifying scenario I had survived many years ago. My mind started to run wild with what was going to happen to me. My mind, on some level, was preparing to re-experience the event that I had undergone with Agatha in her home. This time I did ask who it was. Trust me, I learned my lesson, and a male voice replied, "It's the Avon lady". At that point, I knew it was my partner, but I was so petrified, I had to ask whether it was actually him before I unlocked the door. We had a little chuckle, and of course, I let him in, but when I did, he noticed how much my body had been trembling.

This is an example of the power of the subconscious mind. The incident at Agatha's house in London occurred twenty-two years ago, and it still sends my brain and body into an automatic flight response. The good thing about this is that we can change the subconscious mind, and this is certainly one area that I have to work on to change. I don't want to be living the rest of my life petrified when I am alone in a house and hear the sound of doorbells, that is for sure.

The other positive thing is that if the subconscious mind can be this strong and stubborn with fear and negative events, it can also be used as a potent tool to create more positive outcomes for your life. My example shows how after twenty-two years, I still felt paralyzed with fear in a house alone at night, and that fear increased automatically and dramatically when there was someone at the door. That one incident impressed my subconscious mind on such a deep level, and it was not letting go of this impression. The only way it would let go is with my conscious input to change it. This means that if I impressed my subconscious mind to work for me rather than against me, I would be able to excel easily in the areas of my life that I really wanted to. Once I make that impression, my results will be permanent unless I experience another event with a strong enough level of impact or if I consciously work on changing that paradigm.

How do we change our subconscious mind to benefit us? There are two key factors that impact the subconscious mind. One is strong emotion and the other is repetition. This is why mirror work, affirmations, dream boards, and writing your script of who you would like to become, or how you would like your life to be, work so well when they are done with deep emotion and a feeling of already being there by having that thing that you would like. We do this by using our conscious mind to develop new and positive thoughts and emotions to replace the old destructive paradigm that no longer serves us. If you don't know what your subconscious paradigm is, all you have to do is look at your behavior and your results. Your results always show what is happening at the deeper subconscious level. You will never change your results until you change your subconscious paradigms.

Changing Your Subconscious Mind to Benefit You

This is a simple activity that you could use in any area of your life where you want to get better outcomes but you just don't seem to succeed no matter how hard you try. Another reflective exercise for your Your2Minds journal.

1. Think of an area where you have wanted to improve your results or change your behavior, but it has been difficult to do so. Write it down.
2. Write down the results of behavior that you usually get in this area.
3. What is your mind telling you about this area? Write it down.
4. Write down what you would like to be like in this area. You might have a longer version of this first, and if you have, that is great. Now write down what you would like the change to be in a one sentence affirmation beginning with, "I am so happy and grateful now that…" For example, "I am so happy and grateful now that I feel calm and safe in big homes"; "I am so happy and grateful now that I am earning $300,000 from my business"; "I am so happy and grateful now that my relationships are smooth and amicable"; "I am so happy and grateful now that I am a successful businesswoman." You get the drift. Now it is your turn.

Using the statement "I am" is extremely powerful. Your subconscious believes a statement with the words "I am" in front of it and will automatically elicit feelings and actions to fulfill the words you are saying to yourself. I have heard Wayne Dyer state that the response, "I am that, I am" was the response that Moses received when he asked God to reveal himself as He spoke to him through the burning bush on top of Mount Sinai. So, please be very careful of your thoughts and your mind, and be aware, very aware, when your mind is saying a negative statement after the words, "I am" – cancel that negative thought immediately.

5. Say this affirmation as many times during the day as you can. Say it in the morning and evening in front of the mirror.

6. Make sure you feel emotion when you say your affirmation. It is the emotion and belief that will really impress your subconscious mind. Without adding emotion and belief, you are just saying words that do not have the impact on your mind. Remember, emotion lifts your vibration, and belief shows that you are ready and telling your subconscious to prepare the way for you because it will happen.

7. Say your affirmations for a minimum of ninety days and longer if required. Remember, you have been feeling, behaving, and getting these same results for a long time. It might take a while for your mind to change. Be patient. Be persistent. The change you will eventually see in yourself and your life is worth the effort and persistence. Your life is worth it. You are worth it. If you write your affirmation out every day, that is even more powerful.

The 2 Voices in Your Mind

"Your biggest challenge isn't someone else. It's the ache in your lungs and the burning in your legs, and the voice inside you that yells 'CAN'T,' but you don't listen. You just push harder. And then you hear the voice whisper 'CAN.' And you discover that the person you thought you were is no match for the one you really are."
~ Unknown.

Unless you have done a lot of work on yourself, it is likely that before any decision you make that is a little different or uncomfortable for you, you will have a lot of chatter going on in your mind. It doesn't matter what the decision is – whether it is related to your work, your finances, a relationship, buying a new home, or going on vacation, your mind will probably go off like a machine producing a production line of chatter. You will probably have one side of you telling you that you cannot do the thing that you are thinking about doing. It will tell you that you cannot do it, that you've never done it before, that you're not good enough, that you're not pretty enough, not intelligent enough, not loveable, that you don't have the money, that you really should be saving for a rainy day, that you're crazy for thinking about doing that thing. This is all natural. It is what the mind does. Your mind's function and role is to produce thoughts and to alert you to what could happen, even though it may be wrong.

Often the thoughts in your mind, particularly those that are negative and destructive, come from a place of fear, not a place of love. Your mind is jam packed with the thoughts and expectations or the conclusions it had drawn from your past experiences, whether they were a true reflection or not. But worse still, and what I have learned from Bob Proctor, is that most of these negative and fearful thoughts are deeply embedded paradigms that have nothing to do with us and our potential but rather have been passed down onto us for generations. Yes, that's right. We have been living our life by the beliefs and paradigms that were passed down to our parents from their parents, who were living by the paradigms that were passed down by their parents and so on. What that means is that we have been making decisions and living our lives based on the thoughts and paradigms of our ancestors! Thoughts and paradigms that have been passed down for generations and that have absolutely nothing to do with us!

In addition, we often listen to the expectations of society, our neighbors, the media, and again, the thoughts we are thinking are really not ours. They are not in our best interest, and they certainly do not reflect what we really want, what we are capable of achieving, and what we are worth having. Napolean Hill said, "A man whose mind is filled with fear not only destroys his chances of intelligent action, but he transmits these destructive vibrations to the minds of all who come into contact with him, and destroys, also, their chances."

When I quit my job, there was a battle going on in my mind. One voice was saying, "Well done! You are so brave! How exciting. The opportunity to create a magnificent future awaits!" while the other was saying, "What in the world are you doing? You really must be crazy! What if you fail? Everyone will laugh at you!" The problem was not that I was having these thoughts. It was a massive step to take and one that may have been a little risky. The problem was that I chose to listen to the latter, and that was the beginning of my downward spiral. This voice in my mind grew and turned into a paralyzing anxiety. My passionate, joy filled, happy-go-lucky personality had been hijacked. The voice I allowed to dominate my mind had taken over my natural inner light. My light had not been extinguished. Thank God that no matter what, you can never extinguish that beautiful core essence of who you truly are. It had just been overshadowed and dominated by my fear and anxiety. I fed the fear rather than step into the fear with my own bright shining light.

The concept of our two minds talking and influencing us in two opposing directions can be found in religion. Often these opposing minds are referred to as the angel and the devil talking to us. On one side, we have the angel trying to protect us, trying to sow seeds of love, compassion, and attempting to guide us in the right direction: one that will allow us to see and experience the light, our own inner light, and to experience the life that we deserve. On the other side, we have the devil, who is trying to deceive us, to encourage us to take the road down self-destruction, telling us how unworthy and how much of a failure we really are, that we are guilty, that we will never amount to anything much and will lead us to self-sabotage if we did start to achieve anything.

In more modern theories, we hear about the true self and the ego. The true self is that pure, trusting, and connected side of you. It is the side that comes from love while the ego is that side that lives through a place of fear. The ego will hold onto its identity at any cost, and it will scream louder when it feels you changing and letting go of your old ways. That is why real change requires discipline. When the ego feels threatened, it will get louder, just like when you try to change a deep paradigm, it fights. The ego loves to tell you what you can't do, who you can't be, and it likes to falsely inflate itself in front of others. It likes to attack you, to attack others, and to focus on their faults, real or imagined. It does this because it is afraid. It is afraid of becoming nonexistent, it is afraid of losing its identity, it is afraid of what others think, it is simply afraid in every way. When you come from a place of love, you are liberated from fear because there is no reason to fear. It can no longer paralyze or control you. Love is the light, and where there is light, the darkness fades. Actually, your core essence is perfect, unconditional love. This means that you are perfection at the core. You are the light.

So, whether you call it your two minds, the angel and the devil, or the true self and the ego, they are all different concepts of the same thing. Religious text often explains the two minds by talking about scenarios where one is tempted by the devil, who incites deep suffering that they must endure until they are liberated by the angel or sometimes God Himself. In order to be liberated, however, one must choose the path and want to change.

No one is exempt from having these two minds. We all have them. One of the Universal laws is contrast, so where there is one, there is the other. Although this is true, and it is natural to have some fear, allowing fear to dominate our actions does not allow us to live a free, joy filled, exciting, and full life. Allowing fear to dominate, as we have seen in the above explanation, will lead to self-sabotage and in some cases even self-destruction.

The only way to a free and joy filled life is through love and the emotions associated with love. If you truly come from a place of love, you would first and foremost love yourself. What does it mean to truly love yourself? It means that you would watch your thoughts and ensure that you are planting seeds of love, self-respect, encouragement, and self-forgiveness and eliminating guilt. It means learning about yourself and stretching yourself to fulfilling more of your potential. It means that you are stepping out into fear to live your desires because you know that you are resourceful and have yourself to fall back on when the going gets tough. It means accepting and loving your beautiful body exactly as it is right now, respecting your remarkable mind, and taking care of your needs. It means being in awe of your inner and outer beauty and your unique talents. Interestingly, when you start to love yourself unconditionally, life starts to love you back, and it will bring to you and love you in ways that will leave you in wonder.

As I sat there in Peggy McColl's beautiful cottage admiring Mississippi Lake, Ontario, I asked Peggy what it means to really love yourself, and a new conversation began. We talked about how truly loving yourself is similar to that of loving a child. You love a child unconditionally. You see their beauty, their innocence, their unique talents and abilities, and you encourage them when they fall or make mistakes. You guide them, protect them. You do not scold them when they are afraid, but rather you soothe them and make them feel safe. You notice the joy and light that the child brings to your heart and to the world. You believe in them, and you wish them bright and happy futures. This is genuine and unconditional love. Loving yourself in this way is the path to true self-love.

I will never ever forget the way my grandmother, Baba Nada, loved me. I knew from the youngest of ages that her love for me was unconditional. When she saw me, her face lit up, and she ran to me with her arms wide open ready to wrap me in her tight, warm hug. Her voice changed. She showed me how much she loved me in her tone, and she affirmed her love for me in words. Baba Nada was the only person that I felt loved me unconditionally as a child. She was the only person I felt completely safe to be myself with because in her eyes, I was perfect, and I could do no wrong; through her love, I knew that. I don't remember a time when she scolded us. She never did. She loved us so much that she would always tell us how wonderful, smart, and important we were. We felt important when we were around her. I was always free to be me, and because of the love that I received from this one person, I grew up with that love in my heart and attribute a lot of the confidence that I have as an adult to the love that I received from my grandmother. Her love also taught me how to love myself and how to love others.

Next time the battle with the two voices comes up in your mind, which one will you choose to focus on? Ask yourself if what you choose to focus on is serving you. Ask it if it is loving to you. If not, change it. If it tries to start a battle, because often the ego will fight when it feels threatened, with self-trust, ask your deep core at a soul level what you need to do to be more loving, or to listen to it as opposed to listening to the side of your mind that does not serve you, and that may lead you to self-criticism, punishment, or sabotage.

The 2 Voices in Your Mind Reflection

This short exercise is designed to make you think about how and when your voice talks to you so that you may remember to notice the fear thoughts and change them into loving thoughts. Many of us have not thought deeply about what it means to truly love ourselves, and we may never have reflected on how we could love ourselves more completely. This exercise will help you look at the way you have been toward yourself and then change any destructive or unhelpful patterns to more self-loving and supportive responses.

Think about the following areas, and in your Your2Minds journal, answer the questions after you have reflected on them.

- What are some of the thoughts that come up for you that do not serve you and that come from a place of fear rather than a place of love? Write them down.
- As you go about your day, notice your thoughts. Keep your journal with you, and write down when you notice a fear thought and a loving thought. At the end of the day, have a look at how many of each type of thoughts you had throughout the day. Are you surprised by any of these thoughts? Have you noticed these thoughts previously? How many have you written down? These thoughts have had a major impact on your life, and it is time to start changing them. How

could you change your fear thoughts? Change these fearful and self-destructive thoughts by thinking of a positive affirmation that would serve you. Write the affirmation down as in the previous exercise.

- Take a few moments to think about what it means to really love yourself. Write this description down in detail.
- Think about how you generally treat yourself. Is it loving to you? Are your actions in line with what it means to really love yourself? If not, how could you change your thoughts and behaviors to be more loving toward your beautiful, awesome self?
- Imagine a beautiful child, another person, or animal that you love deeply and unconditionally. Would you talk to them the way you allow your mind to talk to you? Would you treat your loved one the way you treat yourself? If your answer is no, how could you change your self-talk to be more loving and more supportive of yourself? What could you do to treat yourself better, to honor, respect, and value that marvelous, intelligent, and unconditionally important person that you are? Write your answers down.
- Commit to loving yourself every day. Write down one thing that you will do every day to show that you are being loving to you.

A thing that I do when I get caught up in the negativity of my mind, in that constant chatter that tries to beat me to the ground telling me that I am not good enough, I stop. I remind myself to stop everything that I am doing. If I am at home, I light a candle, and I put my favorite soothing meditation music on. I start to focus on the music for a few minutes. I focus on my breath and then my heart and stomach. I move on to opening my heart and solar plexus areas. I open up to God, Source and I feel that fabulous, profound, and powerful unconditional love flow in me and through me. I keep my focus on my heart and Source and let this feeling flow. This is where perfection lives; this is our core. This is the truth. We are all spiritual beings. We have an intellect while we are living in our body. Unfortunately, we are taught to focus on our intellect, and we forget our spirit. It is time to start becoming aware of who you are at your deep core, the real you, the you that has all the answers. It is time to connect with the perfection that lives deep inside you. It is time to allow your spirit to shine bright and bold. During this exercise, I keep focused on my spirit, on my deep core for as long as I need to, until I am ready to get up. Every time I do this exercise, I get up feeling calmer, more relaxed, connected, and ready to go about my day or task at hand with a deep, calm, unshakeable confidence.

I encourage you to introduce a similar exercise in your life. Start off for a few minutes only if you find it difficult to stay focused. When you connect to your true self, to Source, you will feel grounded, peaceful, and inspired because you will have connected to the real you. Everything else is a virus; it is not true. That negative self-talk is not true. It has been lying to you all these years. Through this exercise, you will be guided and understand what your next step will be because this is the place that has the answers.

Remember to write down any new insight, inspiration, or message that comes to you during your little meditation. You will soon understand the beautiful, bright genius that lies quietly within.

Being in 2Minds

"Indecision is the seedling of fear."
~ Napoleon Hill

We all know that feeling when we are stuck between two options, and we find it difficult making a decision. Being in 2Minds about any situation is something that we all have experienced. Being in 2Minds can be stressful, can lead to a lack of sleep, and having the state of confusion impact all areas of our life. The confusion and the feeling of "What do I do?" "What is the better option?", "What is the best decision here?" can be painful.

If you are anything like me, when I have been in this state, if I can't make a decision, I ask another person, "What do you think I should do?" In most cases whenever I am in a situation where I am uncertain about what to do, it is usually during a time of feeling insecure, fearful, or not very confident. Being in an extremely confused state, and the emotion around indecision, can feel like a real nightmare. It is often so much worse than trusting yourself to make the right decision and also trusting yourself that you are resourceful enough to deal with the consequences of that decision.

Being in 2Minds or confusion creates a terrible state of mind. If we are feeling insecure and lack confidence in ourselves, even once we think we have made a decision, we may extend the state of confusion by worrying about whether we have made the right decision. So, the self-torture continues. Even once the decision has been made, you are still in 2Minds about the decision. This thinking does not help the situation.

We all make decisions from time to time that may not have been the best, but in every scenario, there is something learned, some growth happening if we allow it, and we evolve from these situations. Often other more powerful opportunities present themselves from a decision that we may have initially thought may have been a mistake. Continuing the self-torture of being in 2Minds blocks you from growth, self-love, self-respect, and your true infinite potential.

We don't want to live in a confused state of mind. We want to come from a clear and confident state of mind because that creates a more fulfilling life and allows you to make better decisions. It allows you to trust yourself because you know that you will be okay and that you are not afraid to make mistakes, that you trust yourself. It allows you to recognize that you are a marvelous being with a marvelous mind; you really are. Coming from a clear state of mind allows you to develop your will and to focus on where it is that you would like to go rather than where you do not want to go.

A clear mind will show you the next step that you need to take. A frantic mind will only hold you in the same state of confusion, which may lead to further mistakes or a frantic state of stepping out into the dark not knowing what you are stepping into or where it is that you are heading. By living from a clear state of mind, you are showing the Universe exactly what it is that you want, where you are headed, and that you are showing up with your deep inner light with a clear vision. You are showing your worth, your courage, and you are allowing the Universe to respond to you accordingly.

When we are in 2Minds, it is great to ask for advice and feedback. There are many people who have walked the path before us and are where we would like to be. I am sure there are people in your life whose wisdom makes it worth asking them, "What would you do in this situation?" These questions are important because you hear a different perspective. You learn from another person's experience, and through that conversation, an idea or solution may come up in your mind that will help you make the right decision.

Ultimately, we are responsible for our own lives and decisions. So, when you do ask for advice, be aware of why you are asking. Sometimes, we ask for advice because we feel that we can't make a decision ourselves, and it is easier for us not to make a decision and, therefore, we want another person to make it for us. We haven't been taught from an early age how to make our own decisions and take responsibility for them. As a result, we often fear the consequences of our decisions and, in some way, do not trust ourselves to make a decision and to stick to that decision once we have made it.

Being in 2Minds, asking another person to decide for us may provide a solution; however, it is not your own, and therefore, you are giving away your personal responsibility. In this case, you are giving away your power and the right to make your own choices for your life. It means that in some way, you do not trust yourself. You fear making the wrong decision, and you fear the consequence of making the wrong decision. You are not be coming from a place in which you recognize your deep infinite potential and may in some way feel that you may not be able to cope with the consequences of the wrong decision.

If the above scenario sounds like you, and what you may have been doing to date when you have been in 2Minds, please do not beat yourself up. Learn more about yourself. Understand why you have developed this habit, where the fear of not making decisions comes from, and what you are getting from trusting others to decide for you over trusting yourself and knowing what is right for you and your life. While you do this, remember to be aware of the messages that are coming to you from your mind. Notice if they are self-deprecating. Is your mind serving you, or is it sabotaging you? Don't let your mind go to the place where it tells you that you are hopeless and can't do anything right. Just forgive yourself, and practice doing it differently next time. Practice making your own decisions. The more practice you have in making decisions, the better you will become and the quicker you will be able to make decisions in the future. The more you practice, the less time you will spend in states of confusion and being in 2Minds. Notice your mind, and just keep practicing. Remember what it means to learn to truly love yourself?

Sometimes, however, being in 2Minds means that there are big decisions to make and the answer to these may not come immediately. They require contemplation and thought. This is different from the above scenario because the confusion does not come from the feeling of being insecure, fear of making a decision alone, or a lack of self-confidence. They are big and important decisions. These big decisions may be a choice between two great scenarios, or sometimes they may not be so great. It may be a decision around your health, a decision about your relationship, or another member of your family. Sitting with the options and reflecting on them may be required. These periods can be quite stressful, and in some cases, these situations may occur during a time where there are other challenges that you are experiencing, such as grief over a loss or a major change in your or a loved one's circumstances. These are times when we need to tread lightly and allow ourselves the time to feel the emotion and to process all the information that may be coming to you before you focus on the decision. The important thing here is to ensure that you do not let fear and confusion overwhelm your contemplation and delay the decision further. It is also important that you take steps to avoid overwhelming your mind and take daily steps that will get you closer to the right decision. Once you have processed your options, made a decision that you feel is the better option; it is time to let it go and have faith.

Making a Decision When You're in 2Minds

Nobody enjoys the state of being in 2Minds. What do we do when we find ourselves in this bewildered and painful state?

Part A: Is being in 2Minds your normal state?

The first step when you are in 2minds about a situation and decision, you need to ask yourself the following questions: remember to use your Your2Minds journal and to be completely honest with yourself no matter how difficult or confrontational that may be for you:

- Am I confused because I am afraid of making this decision, and do I feel insecure about decision-making?
- Has the pattern of making decisions for me previously led to further confusion or a state of being in 2Minds?
- Am I confused about making this decision because it will be easier for someone else to make it for me?
- Do I trust myself to make decisions?
- Do I trust that someone else would make a better decision than what I would do for myself and my life?

If you have answered yes to any or all of the above questions, I congratulate you for being honest with yourself; this is the first step to changing anything. The next step is to understand why you feel that you cannot make the right decisions for yourself and your life. To know yourself and why you do what you do allows you to move forward. As Lao Tzu stated, "He who knows others is wise; he who knows himself is enlightened." (If you answered No to all the above questions, you can move to part B of this exercise below.)

Remember to write your answers down in Your2Minds journal:

- What is it that I am afraid of in making this or other decisions?
- Where did this insecurity come from?
- What is the cause of my insecurity and lack of confidence?
- Why is it easier for me to give this over to somebody else?
- What could I do to change this pattern in me? Make a decision. Please don't say, "I don't know."

Part B: Steps to help you make a decision when you are in 2Minds

Great! So, now you know why you find it difficult to make a decision. You are ready for the next step. This step is for everyone, whether your confusion stems from fear or it is a decision that requires contemplation. Part B will guide you through a process that assists you in deciding any time you find yourself in 2Minds about anything in your life.

- Sit quietly. Completely relax. Relax your mind, relax your body, and connect to your inner core – this is where the answers come for me. You may want to do the little meditation from the previous chapter to help you connect within.
- Write a short description of your situation and what it is that you are in 2Minds about.
- Write down a succinct question regarding the decision you would like to make. For example, "What do I do about scenario A (insert short description of scenario A here) and scenario B (insert short description of scenario B here)?" or "What is the right decision for me to make between option A (insert option A here) and option B (insert option B here)? You may also have another preference you would like to use for your question.

- Close your eyes, and sit quietly for a few minutes. Focus on your breath, and quiet your mind. Once you feel that your mind is quiet, and you are reasonably relaxed, ask yourself the question that you have written down. Allow answers to flow to you. Do not stop them. Do not get into your mind. Keep your mind out of this. Just let whatever comes up flow through. Use another colored pen (a different color from the one you used to write your question down), and in another color, write down whatever comes to you. Do not analyze the thoughts that come or think that they can't be right or that they are impossible. Just allow whatever appears to you to flow through. Do not block it, and write anything that comes up down on paper in another colored pen.

- Once you have written down all the answers, reread them out loud. Close your eyes again, and relax your mind. Now ask yourself, what is the solution for me in this situation? And in a different color, write out what comes to you. This, as you did above, is a free flowing exercise, so do not let your mind get in the way. Just keep writing. Once you are done, reread all your answers out aloud again.

- Once you have completed the above exercise, put your Your2Minds journal away. You do not need to think about your problem or the decision you have to make until you go to bed. In fact, if you can, try to avoid thinking about it. Put it aside, and concentrate on becoming as relaxed as you can while you go about your day.

- Before you go to bed, go through the responses that you have listed on the paper. You might even want to do the exercise again at this time. This would be recommended if you have the time because you may get a stronger sense of clarification by doing this another time. You might even want to put your list under your pillow. When we ask ourselves a question and do an exercise similar to this one before we go to bed, the question taps into our deep inner knowing as we allow our subconscious mind to do its work and to come up with answers for us. Often these might be the right answers for us.

- Make sure once you have completed the exercise before bed, you let the situation go. Don't think about it. Just focus on relaxing your mind and body and getting a good night's sleep.

- When you awake in the morning, before you get out of bed, write down the first things that come up for you. Some of the things that come up in your mind may not seem directly related to the decision you have had to make. Write them down anyway. Remember not to analyze or let your over thinking mind get in the way. When you have written down your thoughts, you may be pleasantly surprised by the answer. Often after a good night's rest, when you have done this exercise the night before, an answer that feels right to you will appear.

- This exercise may be repeated during a few consecutive nights until you have a strong inner knowing that you have the answer. Sometimes, by looking back at the answers you have written down previously, you may notice that you have had the answer during the previous mornings or that the things you have written down lead to the right answer for you.

- Remember, the clue to this exercise is to relax your mind and relax your body, and let it flow to you without allowing your analytical mind to overtake or sabotage this process.

The Power of **2Minds** Working Together in a Spirit of Harmony

"Again I say to you, if two of you agree on earth about anything they ask, it will be done for them by my Father in heaven."
~ *Matthew 18:19*

It has been written that when two minds gather together with one focus, in a spirit of faith and harmony, that which they are focusing on is guaranteed to manifest. I have experienced this over again in my life. There is something mystical, something magical, that happens when two minds come together. It is written in the Bible (Matthew 18:19) that when two people ask for something in a spirit of harmony, it is granted to happen. There is a certain power in the spirit of two with the same focus and harmony. There is a doubling of strength of will and focus and a magnified lifting of vibration. The vibration associated with the goal or end product takes a quantum leap in energy, and as a consequence, there appears a quantum leap in results. Our actions take on a stronger leap of faith and a quiet confidence because we are not only carrying our desire and dream but also the goodwill, faith, and focus of our partner. This is the strength and power of 2Minds with the one focus working in the spirit of harmony, working to uplift and strengthen and carry the excitement of not only their dream being realized but the dream of their partner. It is a magic that is propelled by genuine care and love, and through this spirit, we have a deeper connection to source.

I have had many experiences whereby I have prayed with a friend or worked toward the same vision or shared my friend's vision and have seen beautifully magnificent manifestations come about as a result. The one experience that I would like to share with you is how a complete stranger, who then became a dear friend, and I put on a challenge to work together for ninety days and the miracles that came from that.

It was January 2016. I was enrolled to do a course in Sydney, Australia. I had a call from a young man who was working for the company that ran the course. Our energy had aligned on that call, and we began talking as though we had been close friends for years. One of the immediate things I noticed about my new friend was his desire to be of service, his professionalism, and willingness to go out of his way to help me out. During that phone call, we began talking about our dreams, our goals, and the challenges that we experienced in reaching those goals. It was one of the most uplifting conversations that I have had with someone whom, before the call, I had only met once briefly. By the end of the call, we promised to do something that would assist each other in reaching the goals that we had discussed over the phone. This exercise was mind-blowing. Not only did our friendship grow, but we really noticed the impact of working in complete harmony with someone who is completely focused on assisting you to achieve your goal. The goals we spoke about that day were the big goals: those goals that are more like dreams, like fantasies. They keep stirring deep inside you, and year after year, they keep coming up, the desire churning, yet year after year, you find yourself not much closer to realizing them. I guess that is why they are called fantasies. They seem impossible, but for many of us, they never stop playing with our desire.

During that conversation, my friend and I decided to undergo an experiment. We agreed that we would choose three goals that were big, that we have had difficulty achieving previously, and that required us to have a complete transformation in that area.

I chose three goals I have had for a long time that, for whatever reason, I could not break through to achieve. My goals were:

- To meet and be in a relationship with my soul mate
- To have a three percent consecutive return on my forex trading account
- To establish my own business and leave the job that I had at the time

These seem like fair goals or dreams to work on, right? The problem was that I had a series of broken relationships. Due to my deep paradigms, I attracted men who couldn't commit. On some level, that would keep me safe, and I did not have to deal with my fear of feeling unworthy or unlovable. It was a big price to pay, however, as I had not experienced a loving, committed relationship for over ten years.

In terms of the forex trading goal, I was new to trading, and I had never even achieved a consecutive one percent return on my investment. Every time I came close, I sabotaged my return by making some silly mistakes.

As for leaving work and going into business, I had never been in business before, I did not have the finances, I wouldn't know how to start, and most importantly, I didn't know exactly what I could offer. I knew deep down that I needed to leave work, and I wanted to work for myself, yet I had no clue whatsoever what this would look like.

So, what my new dear friend and I decided to do was to help each other achieve our goals. When I mean help each other, I don't mean the conventional way. We had to take our action as required to achieve our own goal, but we developed a synergy that would propel both of us forward. It was a little ninety day experiment that we were excited about. We set some rules around this experiment. These rules were:

- For the period of February 1 to April 30, 2016, we will work in a spirit of complete harmony, complete belief, and complete support of our own and the other person's goal.
- We wrote our three goals on one side of a goal card and flipped the card over. On the other side, we had the other person's goals with their name on it. So, on one side, my goal card stated:
- "It is April 30, 2016. I have exceeded three percent profits on my forex trading every month for three consecutive months."
- "It's April 30, 2016. I have set up my business name and my business."
- "It's April 30, 2016. I am dating my soul mate." On the other side of my goal card, it had my friend's three goals written on it.
- Every morning when we got up, we would stand in front of the mirror and say our own goals out aloud with emotion, and we would flip the card over and say the other person's goals aloud with emotion. We had to do this with energy and emotion where we felt ourselves and the other person achieving the three goals while we were reading them aloud. As we did this, we would have a vision of ourselves as well as the other person living the goal, and we had to lift our energy to that level of vibration for ourselves and the other person. It was like we were passing on the gift of this energy or vibration to the other person knowing beyond a shadow of doubt in our mind that they were living that goal or dream here already.

- We would meditate daily for a minimum of ten to fifteen minutes. We would meditate on our own goals and then the other person's goals during this period, and we would send the other person uplifting energy with excitement about them achieving their goal. We would see ourselves and them living with their goal achieved as we did with the affirmations in front of the mirror. It was done. WE HAD ALREADY ACHIEVED THESE GOALS AND WERE LIVING THEM in our minds.
- Throughout the day, we would think about the other person and send them love and positive energy for the achievement of their goal. We would stop a few times during the day and send them and ourselves love and the vision of them and ourselves achieving the goal.
- Once per week we would connect over the phone. This conversation had to be positive, and we would check in to see where the person was at and offer suggestions and ideas about what they might be able to do next. In situations where one of us might have been feeling flat, by the end of the conversation, it was both our responsibility to leave the conversation on a higher vibration excited about our own and each other's lives, dreams, and who we were as people.
- If one person was feeling discouraged, needed some suggestions or advice, or needed to resolve something, they would call the other to talk it through and come to a solution. We always ensured that we left the conversation on a higher vibration than what we were on when we began the conversation.

When we were in the midst of doing this little experiment, there were times when it felt too long, that the three months would never go by, days where we were a little discouraged, and there was also the little fear of it not working. But we continued to get up each time we were down. We had made a commitment and promise to ourselves as well as the other person, and neither of us was going to quit until our 90-day 2Minds Challenge was over.

Our little 90-day 2Minds experiment was a real turning point for me. It created miracles.

We started the 90-day 2Minds Challenge on the 1st of February. I met my partner on February 14th. As I have mentioned, I did not have a great history with relationships, so I was not sure if he was my soul mate or whether it would work out. However, this time I did not let it affect me in any way, I did not question it, I did not worry about it. I just focused on where I wanted to go in life and did not even think about whether this relationship was the right one at the time. I did not entertain the "what ifs'" in a negative way for one second. Somehow the 90-day 2Mind challenge lifted my vibration to a more positive, natural, and free state of mind, and I simply allowed things to flow. Having my friend's energy, support, focus, and total belief in me assisted me to lift my vibration. The daily meditation also helped tremendously. For the first time, I simply enjoyed getting to know this new, wonderful, and, in some ways, remarkable person. Having my new 90-day 2Minds Challenge friend's energy focusing on where I was going and his unquestionable belief in me really helped. The meditations we did also helped because they assisted me in calming my mind and allowed me to enjoy and go with the flow with this new man that I had met.

In October 2017, one year and eight months after my friend and I did the 90-day 2Minds Challenge, the man I met on February 14, 2016 is a big wonderful part of my life. Now if you knew me before I did the 90-day 2Minds Challenge, you would know that this is a miracle. I had been to counseling, to psychics, did affirmations, had been on dating sites, and had probably been on well over one hundred dates. I was never interested, never felt quite right, or the ones that I thought I would give a go couldn't commit or wouldn't commit to me. This is the power of 2Minds working together. Our 2Minds had created a synergy, a vibration that went above and beyond the limitations that I had held for years in my mind.

Regarding my forex trading goal, I decided to learn how to trade because it was something that I knew nothing about, and it greatly intimidated me. The intimidation and fear of trading or trying to learn something new and foreign to me was the major reason I thought I needed to do this. It was time to get very uncomfortable and to challenge my mind in a way that I had never attempted to do before because of my ignorance in the area and my deep ingrained fear and stories in my mind telling me that I could not do something. I also wanted to learn how to give myself other options and have multiple sources of income so that I did not have to rely on the "job." However, shortly after learning a few of the strategies, I discovered that like other areas of my life, I would self-sabotage. I would be close to the percentage of profit that I wanted to achieve for the month, and I would do something silly, like not analyze a trade before I put it in. Consequently, I would lose all the profit and sometimes a little more. I never reached anywhere near that three percent return for one month, let alone for three consecutive months before my friend and I did the 90-day 2Minds Challenge.

The goal of achieving a consecutive monthly profit of three percent return seemed impossible. I knew it wasn't – other people were making a three percent profit and more consecutively, but for me, it felt like too big of a stretch. I remember thinking, "How in the world am I going to do this?" But I had to do it. I had to at the very least focus on it with all my energy because if I did not do this, I could not expect my friend to do the same. For the entire 90-day 2Minds Challenge period, I did a trade analysis every night, listened to webinars, followed the strategies that some experts used, and put in the trades I felt comfortable with. I was focused. I wasn't sure I could do it, but I promised my friend to stay focused, and I did. I cannot even remember what happened month to month, but I can tell you that I achieved a three percent return every single month for the three months that we were committed to the 90-day 2Minds Challenge.

The third goal that revolved around leaving work and starting my own business was the only goal that I did not achieve by the end of the 90-day 2Minds Challenge. However, I was gob smacked when a few weeks after the 90-day 2Minds Challenge concluded, my boss called me into her office to tell me that there was going to be a restructure and that my job would be affected. This was the break I was looking for, and since I couldn't make the decision to leave work myself, the Universe had dangled a carrot in front of me to test whether I was serious about my goal. I did not take the package after that restructure immediately. I waited six months to leave this wonderful organization, but the decision inside myself had already been made there and then. At the time, I did not know what business I wanted to get into. I knew I wanted the option of working my own hours from home and if I could choose anything, it would be working with people to help them achieve their potential. I just did not know how to go about doing that.

So, you can see how the power of 2Minds working in harmony for themselves and each other really works. The three goals that I set out for the 90-day 2Minds Challenge were huge for me. I did not know how they were going to happen. To be honest, I did not even know if they would happen or if this 90-day 2Minds Challenge would work. One thing I did know was that I would not let my new friend down. I was committed to doing this completely and fully, and if my dreams did not manifest from this 90-day 2Minds Challenge, I was certain that his would. I wanted him to achieve his goals wholeheartedly. I felt him achieving this, and I could see him in a greater and brighter light than what he could see himself. I knew with all my heart and soul that my new friend had such amazing potential, and I was so excited about him attaining great success. This excited me. I could not let him down, and there was not a shadow of doubt in my mind that I would. I had to keep focused on my goals for myself but just as importantly for him too.

It was incredible to see the 90-day 2Minds Challenge work. After the challenge, my friend and I stayed in touch. We were so excited about the work we had done together with the 90-day 2Minds Challenge. Amazingly, the challenge did not only bring us the attainment of goals that were a challenge to achieve previously; it brought us so much more. It brought us a great friendship, it brought us the excitement of working together on a project with another person, it brought to us pride that we had created something we had never heard of or done before – the 90-day 2Minds Challenge was our creation from that one conversation we had over the phone back in 2016. It brought us belief, it brought us inspiration of what two strangers could do when they come together in a spirit of respect, belief, and harmony, and finally, it brought us other ideas of what we could do for ourselves and other people. I would love to invite you to find a person, someone whom you know or not, to try the 90-day 2Minds Challenge. If you do it completely with the right spirit as we did, I am sure you will get great results and learn some magical lessons along the way.

As I wrote this chapter, I went back to some of the messages my friend and I sent each other during this 90-day 2Minds Challenge. The most evident thing for me was the high vibration that we created during this period. Just reading some of the messages immediately put me in a higher and happier vibration. The value of this exercise is beyond words. Here are some of the messages we sent each other through Messenger:

March 16, 2016 (7:27 a.m.):

…how are things going with you? I have a feeling you have already hit 2% for the month or definitely close to that :)

I've been a bit slow with trading. Need to pick it up again!!! Been doing lessons online and I put a trade that's not doing so well. I've really got to hit 3%!!!!!!!!!!!!!!!!!!!!!!!!!!'

You definitely will. Patience and consistency. You are learning and will hit 3% this month easily :)

I certainly hope so.

March 17, 2016 (8:54 p.m.):

OMG!!! Something weird just happened!!! I… put in a few trades. One was triggered, and I thought I had to close the other trades which did not trigger. I've been keeping an eye on the one that triggered because it was going up and down and I was nervous… because I can't afford to miss my 3% target. Anyway as I was checking the trade terminal, I noticed an additional 'green' figure that wasn't there before. One of the trades I put in…triggered (without me realizing it) and closed as a winning trade. The two successful trades I put in have given me my 3% profit!!! I think I might close the third trade while it's still in the green to ensure that I lock in the 3%. THANK YOU, UNIVERSE. THANK YOU!!!!! That's two months at 3%, one more month to go and goal number 1 has been achieved!! THANK YOU!! I am so very happy and grateful now that I am a very successful forex trader!! Thank you, thank you, THANK YOU!!!!!

March 17, 2016 (9:28 p.m.):

Just closed the trade. I have come in at 3.38% return for March. I'll stop trading on live account and start on my demo account of the rest of the month!! One more month at 3%!!!!!

March 18, 2016 (10:01 a.m.):

Boom!!! I knew you would do it!! So proud and happy for you!! Killing it! Now time to keep practicing and honing in on your skills :)

Response after I asked my friend for some suggestions around what I should be concentrating on and how I could keep improving myself and my goals:

OK – will do. Thank you again for everything… (my friend)!! I am so grateful to have met you and to be working with you!!!

Honestly, I feel the exact same way :) I am using my day off at redoing and improving my charts…

WE GOT THIS!!!'

March 22, 2016:

Don't think about them (the dream company) getting back to you or when/if it's going to happen. Your job is to create it in your mind and lift your energy/vibration to a place where you're grateful that it is happening. The rest is up to the Universe so let it go and let it do its work for you!!! Sending you massive energy. I know it is going to happen right now for you, and I am thanking the Universe for it!! You go, my friend, keep that razor sharp focus!!!'

Thank you :) I will keep lifting my energy and vibration. I felt disheartened because of the long wait, and it has been influencing my mindset but time to get back on track. I still have to read our goals every day :)

Awesome!!! Just keep focused on where you're going, and the rest will take care of itself at the perfect time.

Don't Give Up!… Let's Do This!… We got this!

March 24, 2016 (8:54 a.m.):

…Remember it's 90% psychology!!! Keep focused, buddy. You're on the right track.

The 90-day 2Minds Challenge

The 90-day 2Minds Challenge is one of the most powerful experiences in terms of committing yourself and committing to another person. Magic really does happen when 2Minds work together in a complete spirit of harmony. Not every day of our 90-day 2Minds Challenge was smooth sailing, and not every day went as planned. But we were committed to ourselves and each other, and as a result, we were uplifted to a vibration that was beyond explanation. We reached our goals, although some took a little longer than the 90-day period, and we developed a very strong friendship. At the end of our 90-day 2Minds Challenge, we were excited. Ideas started to flow through us: ideas that we would not have thought about had we not committed to our 90-day 2Minds Challenge.

Now it is your turn. Whom do you know that you would like to do the 90-day 2Minds Challenge with? Whom do you admire? Who resonates in a nice positive energy? Even if it is someone you may not know that well or someone who you might think won't want to work with you, I challenge you to approach them and ask if they would be willing to do the magical 90-day 2Minds Challenge with you.

When you have found the person whom would like to do the 90-day 2Minds Challenge with you, give them this book, and ensure that you both agree on being fully committed to your goal, to the other person's goals, and to follow the 90-day 2Minds Challenge rules. Again you will need your Your2Minds journal to write out your goals, but I also suggest that you both keep a journal to brainstorm and help each other with new ideas and solutions. Use your Your2Minds journal to record any insights that come to you, any changes in emotion, frustrations, any breakthroughs. By writing you are allowing new insights and ideas to come to you, but at the end of your 90-day 2Minds Challenge, you will be able to read back through the notes you've recorded in your Your2Minds journal so that you may be reminded of how much you have grown through this process and how you have benefited from the 90-day Your2Minds challenge. Now, these are the rules that you and your 90-day 2Minds Challenge partner will need to implement for the whole 90-day period:

- First, write yourselves a commitment letter that you both sign, and keep a copy. There is a sample commitment letter at the end of this chapter. You could use this, or you could make up your version of the 90-day 2Minds Challenge commitment letter.
- For 90 days, you will work in a spirit of complete harmony, complete belief, and complete support of your own and the other person's goal.
- Write out your own three goals (or up to three maximum) on one side of a goal card and the other side of the goal. Write out the other person's goals with their name on it. Write your goals out in the following structure:

It is (insert date). I am so happy and grateful now that I have... (insert goal)...

and on the other side of your goal card, you can have your friend's three goals written on it.

- Every morning read your own goals out aloud with emotion in front of a mirror. Flip the card over, and say the other person's goals out aloud with emotion in front of the mirror. Make sure you do this with energy and enthusiasm. Feel and envision yourself and the other person achieving the goals you have both set out to achieve and have written out on your card. Hold a vision of yourself as well as the other person living the goal, and ensure that you lift your energy to that level of vibration for yourself and the other person. Remember, you are passing on the gift of this energy or vibration to the other person knowing beyond a shadow of a doubt in your mind that they were living that goal or dream here already.
- Meditate daily for a minimum of fifteen minutes. You are meditating on your own goals and then the other person's goals, and during your meditation, you will be sending the other person uplifting energy with excitement about them achieving their goal. See yourself as well as your 90-days 2minds challenge partner both living with your goal achieved. It is done. You are both actually living your dream now.
- Throughout the day, think about the other person, and send them love and positive energy for the achievement of their goal. Stop for few times during the day, and send them and yourself love and the vision of the goal being realized.
- At least once per week, connect over the phone. This conversation must be conducted in a complete spirit of harmony, and ensure the conversation ends with a positive and uplifting energy. Check in where the person is at, and offer suggestions and ideas about what they might be able to do next.
- If one person is feeling discouraged, needs some suggestions or feedback, or needs to resolve something, commit to calling the other to talk it through and come to a solution. Always ensure that you take responsibility in ending the conversation on a higher vibration than what you were on when you began the conversation. If you are the person listening to the setback, remember to keep focused on what the solution may be for your 90-days 2Minds challenge partner; never focus on the problem. Come from a place of understanding and compassion, but always concentrate on where you are going and how wonderful it is that you are living your two dreams or goals.

And if you do get a little unfocused from time to time, think of what my dear friend said to me during our 90-day 2Minds Challenge:

"... *Remember, it's 90% psychology!!! Keep focused, buddy. You're on the right track.*"

The 90-day Your2Minds Challenge Commitment Letter

I… (insert your name here)… dedicate the next 90-days beginning… (insert date here) and ending… (insert end date here)… to the 90-day 2Minds Challenge with my 90-day 2Minds partner… (insert partner's name here). This means that for the next 90-days, I will work in a spirit of complete harmony and focus. I dedicate myself to the following actions for the entirety of the 90-day 2Minds Challenge:

- I will read my goals and my partner's goals out loud with emotion every morning and every night.
- I will meditate daily for a minimum of fifteen minutes on my goals and my partner's goals as outlined in Your2Minds.
- Throughout the day, I will think about my 90-day Your2Minds challenge partner and send them love and positive energy for the achievement of their goal.
- At least once per week, I will connect with my 90-day Your2Minds challenge partner over the phone. I will check in to see where my partner is at and offer suggestions and ideas about what they might be able to do next. I will take responsibility for my vibration and will ensure that I leave every conversation in an uplifting vibration.

I look forward to realizing my own goals and witnessing my 90-day 2Minds partner's goal be realized. I look forward to working in a complete spirit of harmony, and I take responsibility for my actions. I acknowledge that I am here to hold the vision and totally believe in my own goals as well as that of my 90-day 2Mind's partner's goals. I look forward to the growth that we will both experience as a result of this challenge.

Signed: … (sign your name here)…

Date:…

Once you have completed a copy of the 90-day Your2Minds Challenge Agreement, be sure that you send a signed copy to your 90-day Your2Minds Challenge partner.

My2Minds –
Experiencing Depression and Anxiety

*"Character cannot be developed in ease and quiet.
Only through experience of trial and suffering can the soul be
strengthened, ambition inspired, and success achieved."*
~ Helen Keller

Some of you who are reading this book, and who do not know me, might be thinking, "Well it is easy for her to talk. She doesn't know anything about me or my life!" You may be fed up with people trying to tell you that things could be different. You might be thinking, "Sure, in words it does sound nice that I am such an important part of the Universe, but that doesn't give me the answer to how I can pay my bills at the end of the month, or how I can get that dream job, or buy a nicer house for my family." No matter what your situation is right now, I would just like to invite you to keep focusing and saying to yourself:

'… (your name)… did you know if you weren't here, the Universe would literally be out of alignment?"

I am hoping by you doing this, by making this statement a daily affirmation and reminder to yourself, it will eventually resonate, and from that answers might start to come through to your mind about your next steps. There is a solution to all our problems, and unless we choose to start thinking right, unless we choose to start allowing ourselves to connect to our inner light or our source, we risk the chance of being stuck. Once we allow our mind to open up to the possibility that we might be such an intricate, limitless, and important part of the Universe, we start to unravel our inner genius and our creative solutions.

So, in case you are one of those people who may be thinking that it is "easy for me to say," I would like to share with you one of the challenges that I allowed to continue to dim my light throughout parts of my life. I have already shared some of this in previous chapters, but I felt that it is important to revisit this here.

Those of you who do know me know that, in the past, I have been prone to depression and anxiety. It was an on again off again battle for me. For a deeply emotional person, depression can be a challenge. I now recognize that I have a choice. I have a choice as to how I use my mind. However, if you are experiencing depression, it is important that you get the support of a professional to assist you with changing some of the habits of your mind. When you work through some of these patterns with a supportive professional, it often helps tremendously, and if your patterns with depression and anxiety are serious, I cannot stress the importance of your making that appointment. There is help out there from great professionals, and it is there for you to take it so that you can slowly start to feel better.

Coming from a migrant family settling in the working class suburbs of Melbourne had its many challenges as a child, and looking back at that experience, I think that depression for me kicked in at a very young age. My parents were struggling with their battles of being in a country with hardly any family, where they did not know the language, and they were forced to work extremely hard as process workers in local factories. Their focus was on survival.

When I look back as an adult, my parents become my heroes as I could not imagine the courage they needed to make the decision to pack up their humble belongings and leave their village home to go all the way around the world, not knowing when they would see their family again, not knowing anything about where they were going. There was no internet in those days, and they did not have the opportunity to continue their education. Being forced to leave school at the age of fourteen so that they could help their families survive in the harsh post war environment of the southern Serbian village did not leave them much opportunity to learn anything about the world.

My mother told me that the first time she ever traveled to Belgrade was when she met my father. Being the oldest of four children, her duty was to help her parents provide so that the family could survive. She wanted an education and was a diligent student yet was pulled out of school because there was work to be done to feed the family. Learning anything about the world was never granted, yet ironically when she got married, she found herself boarding a plane with her two-year-old child going on a journey to a foreign land she knew nothing about. The only thing I could compare that with today would be to packing your bags and going to Mars not knowing what it would be like, who would be there, not having any finances, not taking anything that you own, not knowing the language that would be spoken when you arrive, and how you would survive. My admiration for my mother's courage to do that is beyond words. My respect for my parents' determination to survive and have a comfortable life once they made it to Australia is enormous. Making something better of their lives, whether that be through hard labor or working like a slave in the factory environment, was what my parents and many of the European migrants in Australia did; as a result of their determination and hard work, we were gifted with the opportunity of an education and a life with endless opportunities. My gratitude to my parents is enormous because of their decision to step way out of their comfort zone, their impeccable courage, and their unstoppable determination that I have had the abundant opportunity, the friendships around the world, and the vision of even bigger and better things to come.

Like most migrant families, we children experienced very challenging times as a result of my parents' massive decision to leave their homeland and travel across the world to a completely foreign land. In addition to the difficulties that the average migrant family underwent, we were prone to some extremely harsh and difficult situations with bullying. Even these days, thinking back to how terrifying it was for me to walk to school and sometimes be at school saddens me. Those experiences were petrifying for me. I was afraid to leave the house, but I had to build up my inner courage to do so. There were many incidences where I left the house and found myself confronted with abuse.

One day I went across the road to visit my friend and was confronted by another neighbor who was a year or two older than me. After we exchanged a few words, I was attacked. I was quite thin with a head full of thick, long hair. I guess it was easier for my neighbor to grab onto my hair and pull the daylights out of it. By then end of the ordeal, she had chunks of my hair in her hand.

Another time my mother asked me to go to the milk bar when I was chased by a couple of girls from the street; one was the younger sister of the girl who had pulled my hair out. They chased me on their bikes and attacked me. I fell to the ground, and the rubble on the road pierced through the skin of my knees. The cuts were deep, as evidenced by the amount of blood pouring out from my knees and down my legs. I picked myself up crying, too afraid to turn back although I was almost just as afraid and humiliated to keep walking to my destiny. I walked all the way to the milk bar to buy that milk, in pain with my knees bleeding profusely and people staring at me with pity in their eyes. These and other experiences of being a child from a newly arrived migrant family led to immense and deep sadness, loneliness, and anxiety as a child and also later on in life.

As an adult, even though I had studied psychology and counseling and went through my own sessions of therapy, there were still times that depression overcame me along with paralyzing anxiety – sometimes this would appear within social settings, sometimes at work, sometimes it would take over most areas of my life. Even with all this study and my ongoing commitment to personal growth, my paradigms were so deep that they simply became overwhelming until I was in a black hole that in a number of situations was very difficult to get out of and would last for many months.

So, I am just like you are. I have one part of me that is very sensitive and therefore was prone to depression and anxiety, and then there is the other side that is happy go lucky and can uplift everyone in the room. When you are stuck in such a deep and dark place, it is difficult to move out of it. I know sometimes it feels like, when you are in this state, something has taken over your body. It is through sheer determination every single day – in some cases, every moment of the day – that I pulled myself out of these periods. It takes effort and will mixed with persistence.

Once you are out of that cloud, you look back on the experience and thank yourself for pulling out of it because you begin to see the beauty of your life again. You start to appreciate it. I discovered, no matter how difficult it was for me, and no matter how much I did not want to accept it, that it truly is my choice as to which of my2minds I will decide to listen to today and every other day for the rest of my life. During those difficult periods, I did not want to accept that it was my choice because it felt too difficult to do anything let alone start to change some of my thinking.

Luckily, I did eventually accept that if I did not take responsibility for my own life, for my mind, nothing would ever change.

The past has no control over me now. Many of us have challenging periods growing up, but I do not have to give those fearful and deeply negative thoughts any control over me today. I know that I cannot and will not waste my God-given potential. If I am such a compelling piece of that bigger Universal puzzle, and if I have that greatness and beautiful light deep within, I cannot afford to go there again. I must use as much of this light, of this greatness, as I possibly can for myself, for you, and for the Universe. It has become both my obligation and my right to do so.

I have learned that it is only by being my authentic self that I could allow others to be themselves, and it is only if I let my inner light shine bright that I could allow you to let your light shine bright. It is only through stepping out and working toward achieving my dreams that I could serve others because by lifting myself up, I can then lift you up.

Again this is a choice, and it requires waking up every morning and reminding myself of the many blessings that I have in my life. Gratitude is the key. Just being alive is one of the many blessings we all have. No matter what is going on around me, there is always, and I mean always, something to be grateful about. This new realization about my life and who I am requires me to focus on connecting to my light and to let it consciously shine throughout the day. It is about feeding my loving and supportive mind over my destructive, fearful mind every day. It requires me to let go of my paradigms and feelings of unworthiness and replace them with the truth. The truth is that, like you, I am worthy beyond measure. I am infinitely worthy. Like you, I am deserving without boundary; I am infinitely deserving. And like you, I am magnificent beyond measure. I am infinitely magnificent.

Now, please put this book down, and read that last paragraph again. Please read it quietly, and then read it out aloud. Read it in front of the mirror. Read it until it resonates deeply within your core. Go to your Your2minds journal, and write down what came up for you as you read this paragraph: what feelings, emotions, thoughts came to you? Sit with how powerful and beautifully profound these words are. Let them sink in. Remember, these words are about the most important person on the planet, YOU.

My2Minds Exercise

The exercise for this chapter is a short yet profound one. It focuses on realizing the truth of who you are when you discover the viruses that have been in your mind possibly for many years. Quiet your mind for a few minutes. Again, you may want to light a candle and play your favorite meditation music while you do this exercise. In your Your2Minds journal, write down the full statement below in a bright, vibrant color, so it stands out. You may want to highlight it or use pencils to make it stand out. Remember to insert your own name in the spaces. Now sit quietly and connect with your heart again, and add any other statement of truth that comes to your mind to those below. You may come up with one or numerous statements. Whatever you come up with is the right thing for you. Now with your arms wide open, say the entire statement out aloud in front of the mirror. You could re-do this exercise by writing out this statement as often as you would like, but remember to keep repeating your statement of truth as many times as you can throughout the day. We want your statement of truth to sink in deeply and find a new home in the subconscious so that you can stop living the lie and start living your deep core truth. This is who you are; everything else is an illusion. It is a lie. Let go of the heaviness of the lie you have been carrying around with you all these years, and start to live the life you were created to live by remembering your truth every single day. Imagine the beauty that you will be bringing to your own life and to the world by living this truth.

You see, the truth is that:

YOU....(insert your name here)... are worthy beyond measure; you are infinitely worthy.

YOU... (insert your name here)... are deserving without boundary; you are infinitely deserving.

YOU... (insert your name here)... are magnificent beyond measure; you are infinitely magnificent.

Part 2

Your2Minds:
A Lived Experience

Mentoring Your Mind

It is a well-known fact that rarely can a person achieve great success without the guidance of a mentor, teacher, or coach. Although there is mention of some of our great and well-known mentors throughout this book, sometimes a mentor or extraordinary leader comes from the most humble and discreet places. In this section, I introduce a story about one of my greatest leaders without whom I would not be the person I am today. The guidance and learning that I received from this great human being will remain with me throughout the time that I stay on this planet in this physical form. Her remarkable example has survived way beyond her years and will continue to do so for generations to come.

You will see, from the story I share, that this remarkable woman had used many of the concepts shared in this book without ever being taught to do so. Through her story, additional concepts are drawn into the picture, such as using your heart, gut, and mind as three parts of an intricate whole that provide each one of us with the innate tools that we require to achieve anything that we set our minds on, even when the odds are against us.

You have these intrinsic tools deep within yourself. They have been provided to you at birth so that you could navigate the path of your extraordinary life, so that you may be guided, so that you may be equipped with the infinite ability to create what it is that you truly desire. You may need to sharpen your tools due to a lack of use, but you have these tools given to you as your birthright.

Through this remarkable woman's lived experience, you will also see the importance of letting grievances go and living from a mindset of love. Letting go and forgiveness means that you are no longer carrying the heavy weight of burden that you've carried all those years, poisoning your mind, your body, and making it more difficult to allow the Universe to work through you and to bring the things that you have hoped for to you. This doesn't mean that you do not express your emotions, such as anger or disappointment. It means that once you have let your emotions out, you let go of them fully, wholly, and completely.

The story you are about to read about this remarkable woman will show you how gratitude for everything in your life, whether it appears to be big or small, and truly accepting and loving your life as it is right now, even though you may not love parts of your life or circumstance that may have crossed your path, leads to fulfillment and joy. It shows an example of how when you choose to turn your mind to gratitude rather than complaining and lack, you realize that you have everything already and that you will never be without as long as you are expressing true and deep gratitude.

This story will show you that by being yourself and adopting the concepts in this book as well as guiding your mind to connect with your heart, gut, intuition, guiding your mind to focus on love over fear or grievance, and guiding your mind to feeling a sense of gratitude, you will naturally inspire others. Also, you will naturally guide them to be their full and complete beautiful and magnificent selves. You may become a mentor to others to liberate themselves.

In doing the work in Your2Minds, you too may want to look at a mindset coach or mentor. It is difficult to change your deep embedded subconscious paradigms alone, and hence it is important to work with someone who will guide you, who can see your potential and can understand your blocks but most importantly be able to lead you through your deep embedded subconscious paradigms to transformation. I hope you enjoy the story of one of the most remarkable women I knew. Most importantly, I hope that the story inspires you to keep doing the work in this book and to change your mindset to one that benefits you rather than sabotages you and your infinite potential.

Baba Nada's Marvelous Mind

*"The most beautiful things in the world cannot be seen or
even touched – they must be felt with the heart."*
~ Helen Keller

I am going to tell you a story of one of the most marvelous leaders, humanitarians, and women that I have been so lucky to have had in my life and to know. The reason why I would like to share this with you is because although this woman was born in 1919, had very little education, and judging from her life experiences alone, most people would have thought she would have no chance of becoming the remarkable human being that she was, her wisdom went beyond her years. This woman had such a strong influence and impact on so many that, even today, fifteen years after her death, the thought of her brightens up the heart. She was so powerful because she chose to use her mind to allow her bright light to shine in her heart, upon others, and across her neighborhood – both the neighborhood in which she took her first breath, a small village in Southern Serbia and the neighborhood halfway around the world, in which she took her final breath, the inner city suburb of Collingwood, Melbourne, Australia. She made an impact wherever she went, and to this day, although she has physically gone, her bright light continues to shine on in the hearts of all who were fortunate enough to know her.

My Baba Nada, Grandma Nada, was probably the most influential, awe inspiring person that I have ever known. This little pocket rocket was wise beyond her years, and despite all the horrific challenges she had been presented with during her eighty-four years of life, she still managed to shine her light on the world around her.

Born in 1919 in Southern Serbia, Baba Nada lost her mother at the age of seven and was left the oldest female in a house that fed nine people in a tiny peasant village called Masurica. At the age of seven, she had to learn all the household duties, usually those that were the duty of an adult. She had to produce the food, by working on the land, she had to milk the cows and ensure that the household of nine had been fed. It was her role now, and that is what she did.

Baba Nada had a scar on her head. You could only see it if you were playing with her hair, and I saw it many times because she loved it when I would scratch her head for her. She would sit there on her chair by the window of my parents' home and bribe the children she had babysat with twenty cents to play with her hair and scratch her head. Although she loved her hair being played with, it was also probably a way to distract some of us because at that time, she was babysitting nine children at once. The children were from migrant families who had to go to work at the local factories, and because nobody else had the support of a grandparent, they all left their children with my Baba Nada.

Baba Nada told me the story of how she got that scar many times. She was working the land, preparing the soil for the seedlings to go in when her younger sister, who had a terrible temper, and she got into an argument; that is when her sister attacked her with the hoe. Although the story was funny the way that Baba Nada shared it, I am sure it would have been terrifying for her at the time that incident had happened. I could just see that child pining for her mother, having a household of responsibilities to take care of, and then running home with blood dripping down her head.

My Baba Nada was born with something truly special about her. A strength of character that I have not seen or experienced in many people. She was unique, and she never swayed or shied away from her own personal uniqueness. She was this tiny woman with true power within, with a personality that would light the whole room and attract people from everywhere and anywhere. A character that saw the best in people, and that is what she would get back from them. She was a bright beam of light that shone way beyond her tiny body. The hardships that she had dealt with in her life may have dimmed that light a little, but most of the time, you could never tell because, boy, her light was bright, and it was very powerful.

I do not know whether this was something that had been refined as her life went on, presenting her with challenge after challenge, or whether it was something that was as strong when she was born. Knowing her, however, I believe that it was something special that she was born with. It was natural and something that you could not fake, and it came from deep within because she connected with it, and she allowed it.

Growing up and living as a peasant farmer in Serbia may not have been easy, but during and after the two World Wars, poverty was the experience of most. The male and female stereotypical roles were also very prevalent. At the age of nineteen, my paternal grandparents had a set-up marriage. I don't know how it worked exactly, but having a well-meaning family, my great uncle set my grandparents up because he felt that my grandfather's family had adequate land to ensure that his sister would be well fed and have the basics in life. He, therefore, did not have to worry about her.

I can't remember how my great uncle met my grandfather's family. I knew that he had served in the Yugoslavian king's army, so he had placements in different parts of Serbia. It was through the travel in his duty serving the king that he must have come to know my grandfather's family as Masurica was very far from Djindjusa, where my grandfather was born and where he lived with his parents and four siblings.

I remember my Baba Nada describing her feelings when she first laid eyes on her future husband – he was tall, handsome, and very nicely dressed. There was another boy that took interest in her in her village, but I guess that was not destined to happen. I struggle with the concept of destiny and making up your own destiny, so I am in two minds about this. Reflecting on my life, I guess that I believe that everything already exists in the mind of God or the Universe, so if it already exists, you have the potential to choose and then lift yourself to the same vibration of the thing you want, but you also need to take action toward it. In the situation of my grandparents, however, I believe that they felt that they had no choice, so they had come to accept that this was their destiny.

My grandparents never had a good marriage. This often made me sad, and even when I think of them today, I really wish that they had the love that they both deserved. They were complete polar opposites. My Baba Nada was a big, strong, bright personality who absolutely loved people, no matter the age, the religion, gender, or nationality. She loved and attracted people from everywhere, and they loved her. She could not live without having people around. She was affectionate. She loved to touch and warm you with hugs, kisses, and would sit there talking with you while she would give you a hand massage. She always gave you her full attention.

My beautiful grandfather, on the other hand, was an extremely quiet, private person. He did not like people. Maybe he even feared them. He did not like having people apart from family come to visit him in his home. He liked his space, his privacy. He did not like to be touched. We all knew that my grandfather had experienced a lot in the war and in life, yet we knew very little about him. He rarely shared anything about himself or his life. This made us a little sad because we all really wanted to learn more about him.

My grandparents' marriage was volatile. Often my Baba's gestures would be met with angry words. She craved love and attention. Her soul was a bright burning light of love and it needed that loving affection. The sad thing was that they were both unhappy, but in their time and culture, separation was never an option.

My Baba Nada told me a story about a time during the war where my father had not yet been born. My uncle had only been a baby. Life had been so tough in her marriage that one day, she decided to take her child and run away. She didn't know how she would do it but she had to return to her birth home as it was terrible for her there. She took her baby and started to go through the forest area of Djindjusa. She thought by going through the forest, she would be able to get to the nearest town without being seen. Remember, back then you did not separate, so had she been caught, she would have been scolded by her mother in-law and possibly disgraced. I am not sure how far she got into the forest when she heard a rustle and sounds that seemed to be groups of people running by. She hid behind a tree and saw in the distance the foreign soldiers. She knew if they had seen her, she would not make it out of the forest alive, and neither would her baby. She sat there silently in complete fear and felt she had no other option but to turn back as soon as she had the chance to safely do so.

Her misery did not only come from a marriage that was empty of love but that of having her oldest child, my uncle, become a chronic alcoholic when they arrived in Australia. What made a person drink so much must only have come from my uncle's internal battles and his internal pain. When he was not drunk, he was the most generous loving, kind, intelligent and beautiful person that you would ever have come across. Unfortunately, he died in his early fifties, and this was another grief that my grandparents had to experience. They found his dead body lying on the floor of his apartment.

Although after my uncle's death, it naturally did take time for me to see my grandmother smile, amazingly she had never lost her light even though she had been grieving so deeply and for a very long time. She was an extraordinary character. A character for whom you would feel tremendous love and understanding in her presence.

It never ceased to amaze me how this elderly woman who knew only a few words of English would have a way with people. After her son died, it had been extremely difficult for them to continue to live in the house that they had been living in during that time because my uncle had lived in the same vicinity, and he would visit them daily. It had become too painful for them to be in there. They lived in public housing. In Australia it may take years to get into public housing because of the long waiting lists; if you already lived in public housing, it could take even longer for you to move into another property.

This did not deter Baba Nada. She went to the public housing office. Don't tell me how she managed to explain her situation; it may have been through an interpreter, but often she just somehow got her message through with her very limited English. Ha, fancy that! A brilliant and determined negotiator who did not know how to speak the same language! She explained to me that she had been told that the wait to be moved into another house would take a minimum of seven years, and unfortunately, there was nothing that they could do to fast track her application. It was no surprise to me that a short period later, I can't remember how long but it wasn't much over one year, she had come to me telling me that they had approved her application, on special grounds (due to the loss of her son), to move to another apartment in a different area. How she managed to do that with such limited English is beyond me to this day. But that is who my Baba Nada was. She had a magical way with people. She was simply incredible.

I will never forgot the day when I went to visit her. It was probably a month before she died. I feel so blessed to have this memory of her. I parked in the carpark downstairs from her apartment block. In front of the carpark was a big block of grass where residents would often sit and their children played. I saw my Baba Nada on the grass talking and hugging a woman whom I had never met. I approached them. The lady had just been shopping and was giving my Baba Nada a bunch of bananas. I hugged my Baba and introduced myself to the lady. When I told her my name and that I was Baba Nada's granddaughter, she said in her broken English, "Maybe your grandmother, but she is my mother!"

The lady had been a refugee from Afghanistan who had recently arrived in Australia with her two young sons. She had nobody here and was escaping a war torn situation in her homeland. My Baba Nada ended up being her only source of connection and family, apart from her two young children, in this new and lonely home of hers. The woman did not know how to speak much English, and my Baba Nada barely knew any English at all. How she did that, to not only connect but to connect at such a deep level that the woman had finally felt some level of comfort, trust, and genuine care without knowing how to communicate, was simply astonishing. I guess the heart speaks a Universal language, and I knew that Baba Nada always spoke from the heart and connected from the heart. People know when they are loved, when they can trust, when they are genuinely accepted. They can feel it. We can connect no matter even if we come from worlds apart because we all have the Universal soul language of the heart. And Baba Nada proved this to be true.

So, why have I felt the need to write an entire chapter of a book titled Your2Minds about my grandmother? Although my Baba Nada truly was one remarkable human being, and she is the person whom I could thank for the confidence I have as an adult, what does this story have to do with the purpose of this book? Well, with all the difficulties and hardships that my Baba Nada went through in her life, many of which I have not included in this book, she had a choice. She could have easily become a sad and bitter person. Experiencing the difficulty of living in an environment where she did not know the language, the culture was very different, the values of society were foreign as were the people, she could have easily chosen to lock herself away at home and be a victim of her circumstances. She could have complained about not knowing the language, about the people being different, about how much she had missed her home county. Having had such a difficult marriage, an alcoholic son who would often become abusive and abrasive, and eventually, losing her child, she could have easily become depressed, and who would have blamed her? This would all have been justified and fair in her situation.

Baba Nada had hypertension, very high blood pressure, and there were times when she complained and talked about her deep pain and grief, but her light and her belief in people, in God, in life never diminished. She allowed her pain and grief to be present and to be with her, but she did not allow the flip side of her mind to take away her spirit, determination, and light. Her experience may have dimmed it for a while but not forever.

Looking back at Baba Nada, she did know the secret to life. What's the secret? you ask. There were a number of attributes that my Baba Nada had. She was continuously grateful, she was an optimist and would focus on the positive in all areas of life, she was authentic and not afraid to be herself, she didn't allow fear to take over, and even during her most difficult times, she held onto her strong faith, a belief or conviction. She was not a religious person in the sense of going to church regularly, but she knew in her heart beyond any crumb of doubt that God was looking after her, and she was always so grateful. She would thank God that he brought her to Australia, she would thank God for her wonderful lifestyle, she would be grateful for her health, she felt wealthy, and she knew for sure that she was protected and given all that she ever needed and more.

It's interesting; my grandmother lived on a pension, yet she always had money. She lived on a pension, yet she was always so generous with her love and her money. One day we were on a tram together, and there was a woman sitting beside us with a pram and a beautiful toddler in it. My Baba Nada started to play with the baby and to connect with the baby's mother. As we were leaving, she looked in her purse and pulled out a $5 note and gave it to the child. The mother's face was so surprised as this was a complete stranger giving not only love but the gift of money to her child. Her face lit up. This is not the first time I had seen my Baba Nada do this. She was a generous giver, always selflessly giving love, an uplifting word, gifts of food, and even money.

Although she lived off the old age pension, not once did I ever hear her talk of lack or that she did not have. She was full of abundance in every way. She was sad but not bitter about the marriage she had dreamed of having but never had, and although it was excruciatingly painful, she was never bitter or spiteful about the son that she lost or the pains of her life. Somewhere in her mind, she decided to let her light shine, to focus on the love that she had received with certainty from God.

I would often hear her say "I am not afraid of dying, I could go today, and when my time comes, I only wish that I go quickly rather than lose my dignity and be a burden on others." Her wish was granted. Her belief and conviction and faith in source had given her that wish. One day she woke up with a terrible headache that grew stronger. She called my father explaining that she wasn't well and that he needed to go over to see her. When my father arrived, he found my grandmother lying unconscious on the ground. My beautiful Baba Nada had died that night quickly and easily.

The discussions around gratitude, belief, and attracting abundance into your life through these principals have only recently become popular. A lot of people are talking about how gratitude has impacted and changed their life for the better. I guess I was fortunate. I had lived these through my Baba Nada, a woman who was wise beyond words.

About a year before my grandmother's death, she told me that a young Macedonian man who would clean their apartments would come by and visit her. This was something that she had looked forward to because she loved to talk, and with him, she could speak Serbian. It is a similar language; therefore, they were able to communicate easily. They developed a friendship. He would visit her, have a coffee, and a rakija (Serbian homemade plum brandy) and a nice chat. She would bring him up to me quite regularly. She developed a nice bond with her new friend and was also looking forward to meeting his wife and family. For some reason, she felt that I may have known him, but Melbourne is a big city, so I never knew why she thought that. She wanted me to meet her new friend, and I too was looking forward to that. I thought that I would finally meet him at her funeral, but he did not attend, so I just resigned myself to the fact that I wouldn't ever meet him with some disappointment.

A few weeks after my Baba Nada died, a colleague came to my office door. As she entered and was about to say something to me, I had this strong realization. I jumped up and said, "Oh, my God, your husband is the man that my Baba Nada had been talking about!" I had been working alongside this beautiful woman for years yet had no idea that we were connected in this way. I asked her to bring her husband in so I could meet him. After reminiscing about the remarkable woman that my Baba Nada had been, he left saying, "When your grandmother died, the lights in Collingwood died." Wow! This is the impact that this small pocket rocket who did not know the common language had on the entire neighborhood and community within which she had lived.

My Baba Nada was so powerful, she brought light to the entire neighborhood only because she let her own light shine. She was a shoulder, a comfort, and person who was naturally able to bring out the light in the person sitting beside her and this was only because she let her own light shine bright first and foremost. She could not have done this if she had chosen to hide behind her fear, her pain, or her grief. Had she chosen to be dim and miserable despite having every reason in the world to feel that way, her impact on others would not have existed. The power of choosing which of Your2Minds you will use. A great example of Marianne Williamson's words (which I have dedicated Part 3 of Your2Minds):

> *"As we let our own light shine, we unconsciously
> give permission to other people to do the same.
> As we are liberated from our own fear,
> Our presence automatically liberates others."*

The Baba Nada Let Your Inner Light Shine Reminders

"Budi dobar drugome, i bices dobar sebi."
"Be good to others, and you are being good to yourself."
~ Nadezda Mihajlovic (Baba Nada)

There was so much that all who knew the great Baba Nada had learned. She gifted many with her great wisdom and generosity. By living this way, she also brought herself some joy. The following are examples of how this wonderful woman lived. By trying to adopt some of these ways of living, you too will be able to add more joy into your life.

Your3Minds –
Let Go of Your Mind and Live from Your Heart

*"The intuitive mind is a sacred gift and the
rational mind is a faithful servant. We have created a society
that honors the servant and has forgotten the gift."
~ Einstein.*

My Baba Nada was a natural at living from her heart. I believe that this is why she was such a great negotiator. She did not let language barriers deter her heart's desires. She did not let fear get in her way. She connected through her heart. By the time my Baba Nada died, the entire shopping district on Smith Street in Collingwood, Melbourne, had known her. She left a mark. Because she allowed her heart to guide her, and to feel and connect with others without fear, she was able to bring out the light in others, even a beautiful refugee woman from Afghanistan who had experienced the most difficult time. Baba Nada left a legacy that will go on for generations.

"Now that is a bit of a twist," I hear you say. "I thought this book is about our minds and not our hearts." You're right. But when I decided to quit my job, it was my heart that was craving something more and my gut that was screaming out to me telling me to quit. It was then my mind that took over, and eventually, when I finally got out of my own way, the ideas started flowing through from the ether. So, in other words, my intuition directed the decision, my negative mind was feeding into the fear and preventing me from making a decision, my intuition was getting stronger, and when I finally let my positive mind be guided by my intuition (my heart and stomach), they all came together and ideas flowed, work came to me, everything that I needed flowed into my life, and I used those ideas guided by my heart and my gut to take the next steps, one of those being the writing of this book.

Quieting the chatter in your mind, and letting your heart guide you are important because it allows us to connect with our intuition.

Living through your heart, or letting your heart guide you, means we are guided by love, we are living with passion, we are driven by desire, and we are eliciting the feeling of joy and excitement to be alive. We start to feel alive. We have purpose, and we have vision, and although we do not know how our heart's desire will be realized, we are excited knowing that that which we desire is being shaped and is right here, right now. We just need to open up and let it in.

Let's get even deeper here. Are you ready for the next twist? Well, what I have just said is evidence based. Science shows that there are neurotransmitters, ganglia, proteins, and support cells in the heart that are also found in the brain. The extensive research by the HeartMath Institute shows that this is a fact. Research from the HeartMath Institute also indicates that our 'heart brain' acts independently of our cranial brain and has a large range of sensory capabilities.

Furthermore, there has been research on the stomach that indicates that this organ shares the same neurons as the brain, and it also has an intuitive function. This means that we might have 2Minds, but we actually have three organs that share an intelligence like the brain. Of course, the function of our brain is different from that of the heart and stomach, but when these three amazing minds work together in coherence, to guide each other, without the ego or the negative chatter of the mind taking over, we can use them to guide our dreams and desires. Our brilliant brain's function is to keep us alive through the thinking functions, through leading some of the functions of our body, and through the fight or flight response. It allows us to process our day-to-day tasks, to remember beautiful memories, to compose and to listen to beautiful music, to analyze and to assess, to solve problems, to read a book, and on it goes, but you get the gist, right? Apart from the obvious functions of our magnificent hearts and stomachs, to pump blood throughout our bodies and to break down and digest food, and because it is not their function to analyze, these organs are able to sense and feel things that may not be explainable to the brain.

My father, who is deeply connected to my brother and I, has an incredible ability to know when we are in trouble even if we are miles apart. It is his natural instinct. He will dream about us but also feel it in his heart or stomach when something is not right with us. My brother had a terrible car accident many years ago. My father knew that something dreadful was going to happen to one of us. He had a dream the night before but could also feel it in his stomach the day after the dream. When I lived in Japan, I woke up terribly ill early one morning, as I got back to my bedroom from the bathroom and lay my body on the tatami floor mattress. At six o'clock in the morning, the telephone rang, and it was my parents. Again, my father knew that there was something wrong and had to call me to find out. Japan is only two hours behind Australian Eastern Standard Time, and they had not once ever called me so early in the morning. So, how do you explain my father's ability to know when the two of the most important people in his life are in trouble? How does he feel that in his heart and gut? How does he dream about that? Intuition. Intuition is real, and those neurons in the heart and stomach explain its function.

The emotions we feel and the state we are in internally radiates externally into the ether. We are predominantly energy. Although we can see, feel, and touch our physical selves that physical self is made out of energy, and there are strong currents of energy flowing throughout our bodies. The energy from our body radiates. The vibration of the heart radiates farther than the brain. According to the HeartMath Institute, our heart emits a strong source of electromagnetic energy corresponding to our emotions, and this field, or the electromagnetic current from our heart, can be measured several feet away from our body. Moreover, the HeartMath Institute research also indicates that by feeling positive emotions we could increase the brain's capacity to make good decisions. Now isn't that just astonishing!!! This is YOUR HEART that we are talking about here.

Your heart knows. But if we are not using our mind to work in coherence with the heart, your mind can undermine the direction in which your heart is telling you to go. If you keep using your mind to ignore your heart, the voice of your heart softens to the point where you can barely hear it. And I don't care what anybody tells you. You cannot be a joy filled person if you are living this way.

I hope that you realize that this is powerful stuff. It is not just some crazy Aussie woman talking to you about the 2Minds, or two voices in her head saying this. This is actually scientific evidence. Your heart has thousands of neurons that can also be found in your brain. Your gut has thousands of neurons that can also been found in your brain. Next time you have that gut feeling or your heart is yearning to do something, listen to it. Don't just listen to it; learn how to work with your heart, gut, and mind in coherence, and take action.

Let's take this one step further. The stronger the emotions coming from your heart are, the stronger the vibration that is exuberating from your heart. Remember, it is now known that your heart radiates a powerful source of electromagnetic energy, and this energy can be felt outside of your body. We all have experienced this. You know that feeling of walking into a room, and you can feel the discomfort in the air. You know that uncomfortable feeling when you feel like you have interrupted something, something has just gone down, and then you find out that there had been an argument.

You could literally impact someone else's life by vibrating on a higher heart frequency. I believe this is what happened with our 90-day 2Minds experiment with my friend. I also believe that is how my Baba Nada managed to light up the life of so many people and her entire neighborhood. It was how her desire to move from one public housing property in such a short period with barely any understanding of the English language had manifested, and in a bureaucracy where it took up to several years to move. She made an impact, and she genuinely connected with her heart.

What does this mean for you? If you were able to follow your heart and focus on what it is that your heart is guiding you to do, lift your heart vibration to that level and beyond, with sheer focus and with the use of your positive mind, your heart vibration will be stronger, and it will more easily reach the people and things that you would like to manifest. It is sure to bring your dreams to you a lot quicker. It also means that if more of us tap into our hearts and lift our heart vibration, if more of us were living on purpose, in joy, we would be able to lift the vibration of our amazing planet and eventually create a more peaceful planet for all. That's just a thought, but it is a powerful concept that is worthy of contemplation.

As for the gut, I was astonished to find when I looked into the brain and gut that they are connected by a complex and thorough set of neural pathways and hormones. Some people refer to the gut as another brain, so next time you have that "gut feeling" telling you to stay away, or telling you to jump on that opportunity, listen to it! Next time your gut tells you to do something illogical, get your negative mind out of the way, and step out. Even if it is one small step; take the first step. Act on it. There will be fear, but that is okay. Fear is a normal emotion that comes up whenever we are about to do something we have never done before. The important thing is that you step into the fear and walk through it rather than let the fear incapacitate you. What my Baba Nada did was illogical. In order to go and meet with the Office of Housing staff several times until they provided her with her new home even though she did not know how to communicate well in the same language, she knew how to connect with her heart while not letting her negative mind tell her to stop trying because she did not know how to speak English.

Express Your Emotions

So, we have heard the wonderful and loving side of my Baba Nada, but don't think that this incredible woman was just a sweet and lovely old grandma. She was what I described earlier, a pocket rocket, strong and determined. Yes, Baba Nada was one hell of a loving sweet woman too, but she was not afraid to express her emotions. When she was angry, you knew it. She would tell you how she felt, or her silence would show you that she was angry until she was ready to express it. Most of the time however, once she was done, she was done. She very rarely held grudges or brought up unfinished business.

She spoke about how she was feeling. She trusted people, so she would speak to them about the hardships she felt, particularly around her marriage and son. This allowed her to unload. She did it in a way that was not draining but a way that would draw you in to listen and understand. I guess that is what she also gave out to the world: a listening ear and a compassionate and understanding heart.

She was a strong character but one that was authentic. She did not fake her emotions. What you saw is what you got. She would cry when she was sad and grieve when she felt the grief. She would speak about her loneliness, yet it was hard to imagine that she would feel lonely for long because of her ability to connect and attract people. Perhaps her ability to express her emotions was one of the reasons why she lived a full and healthy life up until the age of eighty-four.

The message here for us all is that this book is not about always being on a high and happy but more about being genuine. Emotions are a part of being fully alive, and when we don't express them, we are prone to becoming mentally and physically ill. Express your emotions. Let them out. It is important, but don't allow the negative emotions to prevent you from living a full life. You are in control of your mind, so ensure that when you are kicked by life, you do not stay down. Let it out, and then let it go. Move on, and always remember to give any person who has hurt you love. This may sound irrational and difficult, but letting go, moving on, and giving the other person love allows your mind to be free from grudges, negativity, and the weight that grudges, negativity, and anger can bring.

Express Gratitude Every Day

Although Baba Nada was living on Social Security, she thanked God and was truly and deeply grateful for her wealthy lifestyle. I have never ever, not once ever, known my grandmother to be out of money. If she was, she hid it well. Whenever she would see her grandchildren, she gave them money. She gave money to children although she did not know them, and she lent money to anyone who asked her for it. Amazingly, when she did lend money, people would return it honest to their word. If I needed some extra cash when I was growing up, Baba Nada was the one I went to. She willingly and lovingly gave to us. She never allowed her children or grandchildren to return the money that they had borrowed from her. She gave it in joy. She was a generous giver in every way.

Baba Nada was not only grateful about her wealth, she was grateful about almost everything, apart from her marriage. She would constantly and full heartedly say that she was so grateful to God for bringing her to Australia where she no longer had to work the fields, she was grateful for her health, she was grateful for her family.

The joy in my grandmother's heart when she saw her grandchildren was out of this world. As a result of her loving heart, and her gratitude to have had a granddaughter, I was fortunate enough as a child to feel that someone cherished me, that someone in my life loved me unconditionally, and that someone in my life thought I was simply perfect. I cannot convey in words what an incredible impact that this had on me. I would not be half as confident if I hadn't had this special woman in my life.

Baba Nada had been so grateful in her mind for everything that she had that I am sure she felt that she lived like a queen. Ironically, she was like a queen, a queen in many people's hearts.

Live with Faith. Live with Conviction.

Baba Nada was not one to pray or to strictly follow religion as it had been set out in the Serbian tradition. She respected her tradition and religion, but she did not necessarily need to be at church every week to show that she had conviction. Her conviction was inside her, and her way of praying was through gratitude and talking to God in her own way. Baba Nada did not just believe in God; she was convinced. Her faith was beyond any shadow of a doubt, and in her mind, she knew that she was guided and looked after. Her conviction had survived the Communist regime of former Yugoslavia that had taken over after World War 2. It did not matter to her what had been going on in her neighborhood or in the society in which she lived. Her faith was so strong that her external environment did not matter, and as a result of this, somehow her external environment always worked out well for her.

Baba Nada dreamed of a better life of living somewhere in which life was not only about survival. Times were tough for peasant farmers living in former Yugoslavia after the war. It was a daily battle for survival. When you spoke with her about migrating to Australia, there was no doubt in Baba Nada's mind that it was her faith and conviction that led her and her family to the "lucky country."

I hear Bob Proctor talk about conviction all the time. He speaks of Napoleon Hill saying that if you want to realize something, you must first believe that it will happen. If you do not believe, if you do not have faith, you are leaving yourself to sheer luck, and chances are you will never realize your dream. There is a magic that comes through faith. It exerts confidence and strength, and it will show you the way. An example of Baba Nada's conviction was seen throughout her actions. She would never allow fear to stop her because of her faith and her conviction that things would work out the way that she needed them to, and in most cases, they did. If you know what you want and believe that you can achieve and take action toward it, it will be yours to have. As the classic quote from Napoleon Hill says, "Whatever your mind can conceive and believe, it can achieve."

Have an Open Heart. Love Others.

Baba Nada's love for people is beyond any that I have ever experienced. She was guided by her love. She did not fear people; she loved them. Although she was not perfect, it was rare to see her with emotions of anger, jealousy, or hatred. She was led by love. Because of this love for people, she had an extraordinary ability to connect at a soul level. She had the ability to uplift and to be a friend to all, no matter what they were experiencing. Her inner light guided her, and interestingly, the light had multiplied. I guess by loving others, and giving with a generous heart, she unconsciously had her own needs met. Her own problems may not have appeared to be as big or to matter as much. It was the classic "Do to others as what you would have them do to you." ~ Luke 6:31

By living with an open heart and loving others, by seeing the best in people, and connecting with people, we lift our own and the other person's vibration. We are more likely to be living in a state of coherence and unconsciously sending that out into the world. It also means that our body is more likely to be functioning in a state of coherence. This adds to our feeling of overall wellness. It is important for our psychological wellbeing, therefore our mind and our physical wellbeing. We are social beings, and connecting at that deep level is a natural state. By connecting and seeing the best in others, we are more able to see the best in ourselves; we are more likely to be joy filled and at peace. By sharing someone else's joy, we increase our joy.

The negative emotions of resentment, jealousy, anger, control, and hatred do not serve us. They don't harm anyone but ourselves. These feelings do not only have a negative impact on your mind, but they also destroy your peace of mind and can have a terrible impact on your psychological and physical health and wellbeing. It simply is not worth it. Remember, feel it, let it out, and let it go. Forgive yourself first and foremost, and forgive others. Why live burdened with terrible baggage? We cannot control other people's behavior. We only have control of our minds and our lives, so live lightly, live fully, and cut that terrible and unnecessary burden. Always remember what you give out must come back to you, and you simply don't need this crap. As Baba Nada would say, "Cuvaj drugoga i Bog ce tebe da cuva" (Look after and care for others, and God will look after you!).

Baba Nada's open heart soothed. It uplifted, it connected, it laughed out loud with the other person (boy, she was fun!). It looked the person in the eye, and it connected on the deep level of their soul. Although she loved the person she saw in front of her, she would connect deeply with their soul. This is powerful because when you connect with the soul, you are connecting to innocence, purity, and perfection. You cannot connect with another person at a deep level by preaching what they "should be, do or have," or trying to control them, by being resentful, hostile and angry or thinking of the things that the person has done wrong or the mistakes they have made. When the soul speaks, it says that we are all one, we are perfect, and we are innocent because that is exactly what the soul is. There is no way that a person could not feel uplifted or not heard if you have truly connected to them on the soul level. That is why people always felt important when they were around Baba Nada. She left them feeling so much better about themselves and about life itself.

Baba Nada knew how to have fun. She would laugh out loud, have a little drink here and there, and have a joke. What is life without fun and laughter? It brings us joy, and life is meant to be joyful. I would like you to have fun with this too. What could you do to relax and have more fun?

Don't Be Afraid to Show Affection.

In today's society, we have been bombarded by images that illicit fear. Neighbors are no longer talking, and we have developed a mistrust of anyone who may be different or who isn't in our inner circle. We are quick to judge and don't practice stepping in another's shoes.

Baba Nada's warmth came not only from her light but also from her affection. So, this is a short and sweet one: live your life with the beauty of affection.

Have a Generous Spirit.

Baba Nada's spirit was generous in every way. She gave freely and willingly with joy. She gave through her bright beautiful light, she gave by being herself, she gave by connecting with people, listening to their sorrows, she gave through love, she gave through her affection, and she gave by giving material things too. She gave to strangers, she gave to family, she gave to the world, yet she always had. She had a passion for people and a passion for life. She never did without anything.

Through giving we are also receiving. Baba Nada gave so much with a pure and authentic heart. She gave because that is what she loved to do. Unexpectedly, however, she was also receiving. She was very abundant. She felt abundant, and she never did without. She felt that she had everything she needed.

The love, care, and respect that that woman received was incredible. It flooded from everywhere. She felt looked after by all. By giving so much, she received joy, and her light would shine brighter.

Give with an open and loving heart. Give because deep in your heart you want to give. Give because you already have everything. Give because through kindness and giving, we are creating a better world. Give because through genuine and loving giving, you too will receive love, joy, and generosity. "Give and you will receive." – Luke 6:38

Give but remember to also receive because you cannot truly give unless you are also open and willing to receive. The two are of the same thing really. What you give out will come back to you in abundance.

Be Your God Darn Self!!!

Baba Nada was unique. She was not like any other woman her age that I had ever met. She was never afraid of being her true self. She was comfortable in her own skin. She was as charming as you could get, and she would use that charm when she needed it. She was sweet and generous with her love, yet her loud and passionate voice could be heard from outside her house. She was occasionally angry but was never afraid of being vulnerable. She was old fashioned and traditional in some of her ways, but her wisdom exceeded tradition. She was living in a foreign land far from her birth country, yet she did not let fear control her. She would connect and get her message across. It may not have been with ease, but it certainly was with heart and with trust. Baba Nada was her God darn self. She never contemplated being anyone else. She was authentic, and that is where her strength came from. She never allowed her mind to tell her that she was not enough the way she was; her mind was free from the anguish of having to be something that you are not.

We are all born unique, and each of us has beauty in our own uniqueness. Yet somewhere we have picked up the message that we are not enough the way we are, so we mistakenly try to be something that we are not. We try to be liked, try to fit in, try to please by hiding our true and authentic selves. We have been hurt in the past, and for some reason, we related that hurt to not being good enough the way we are. We try so hard and eventually may even forget who we are.

Baba Nada's strength came from her unpretentiousness. She was who she was. She was her unique self. Isn't it interesting that often we try to be someone else so that we are liked, yet when we are trying to be someone else, we are nowhere near as interesting or as beautiful as we are when we are relaxed and happy in our own skin. This is where our real strength lies, quirks, idiosyncrasies and all. We are born perfect in our imperfection. Our uniqueness is what makes us attractive. It is where that light stems from. By hiding your true self just to be liked, you ironically attract people who you need to keep exerting unnecessary energy to be accepted.

Wouldn't it be easier just to relax and let your real self flow out in all its beauty and glory? Don't be afraid to do this. When you are able to relax and be you, life will complement you with ease and with an energy that attracts to you the quality of relationships, work, and life that you deserve. Respect will flow to you because you are in flow and brave enough to be you and nobody else. Besides all that, how much fun and freeing would it be to let go of the worry and burden of trying to be someone you're not? You can fly free and be your magical, mysterious and unique self. Remember when your critical mind starts to try to take over and tell you that you are not good enough to be your true you or that the real you is boring, a failure, ugly, or unworthy, gently tell that mind to move over because it has been wrong all this time. You now understand your true worth, and you are ready to let that light of yours shine bigger and brighter than ever, baby!!

Part 3

Stepping Out of Your Mind to Find Out Who You Truly Are

Let Your Deepest Light Shine

"Your playing small does not serve the world."
~ Marianne Williamson

I wanted to conclude this book, *Your2Minds*, leaving you with a similar message to the one when the book began. I wanted the conclusion to leave you in the state of magnificence because it is critically important that we realize who we really are and that within us lies a well of glory, of power beyond what we had ever imagined. The message fits nicely with the preamble and Bob Proctor's message to us about who we truly are.

This is a similar message to Bob's; we tend to dim our light because we are not aware of it or we fear it. This verse from Marianne Williamson's book *A Return to Love* so clearly and powerfully expresses who we truly are. It also shows the contrast of the 2Minds – one being that of fear, which keeps us being small, and the other being that of love, which shows the brilliance and perfection within each of us when we choose to truly love ourselves and focus on our truth in our mind rather than our negative self chatter.

"Our deepest fear is not that we are inadequate,
Our deepest fear is that we are powerful beyond measure.
It is our light, not our darkness that most frightens us.
We ask ourselves,
'Who am I to be brilliant, gorgeous, talented, and fabulous?'
Actually, who are you not to be? You are a child of God.
Your playing small does not serve the world.
There is nothing enlightened about shrinking so that other people won't feel insecure around you.

We are all meant to shine as children do.
We are born to make manifest the glory of God that is within us.
It is not just in some of us, it is in everyone.
As we let our own light shine, we unconsciously give permission to
other people to do the same.
As we are liberated from our own fear,
Our presence automatically liberates others."
~ Marianne Williamson
A Return to Love: Reflections on the Principals
of A Course in Miracles

I discovered these precious words when I first read Marianne Williamson's book in 1994. They have stuck with me since then. I have them on the wall in my home as a reminder to myself, and to all who visit, of who we truly are. Even though they have been on my wall for many years, I have to look at them frequently to be reminded of that true essence residing in each and every one of us.

Ms. Williamson's words are eloquent yet deeply true, resonating with our deepest core. Take the time to read and reread these words.

Let's look at the words, and let's examine them. As you read the words, tap into your core self, your spirit, and sense your feelings and what they might be telling you.

"Our deepest fear is not that we are inadequate,

Our deepest fear is that we are powerful beyond measure

It is our light, not our darkness that most frightens us."

Somewhere along the journey of our unique and individual path in life, something begins to dim our sacred and natural light. Often this starts to happen in childhood when we are bombarded with messages telling us to be humble, be quiet, we can't have this or that, who are we to think we will be that star we so deeply dream of becoming? Sometimes, these messages come from our parents. Sometimes, they are from teachers or other children. Many of us may have experienced traumatic events, such as abuse, family violence, or bullying. Regardless what your experience in childhood was, whether it was positive or negative, most of us somehow end up growing up with our light needing to be buffered as it has dimmed but never completely extinguished.

Sadly, these messages don't only come to us only as children, but we hear them as adults too. As women, we are constantly bombarded by the media about how we should look and what we should be like to be "good enough." We are bombarded with images of a beauty that has been so tweaked by Photoshop that it is beyond any realm of reality. It has made us forget that we are all beautiful. No one can be more beautiful than the other, particularly when we let our inner light shine. We may all look different, however, when we let our own unique light shine. When we feel the deep love and respect for ourselves, for others, and for life, we are all equally beautiful. We are beautiful in our uniqueness and diversity – no age, dress size, or eye color could take our true beauty away. Every single one of us is far beyond good enough. We are infinite, exceptional, sexy, worthy beyond measure – it is our nature, our deep natural state. These stereotypes only try to install this false feeling of lack to have control over us. They do it because we have forgotten who we truly are at our essence, and as a result, we have given them our power. Unfortunately, they do it because they can.

Women are not only bombarded with stereotypical and unrealistic expectations about what it is to be so-called "beautiful" but who we should be in the workforce, as people, and as mothers. Mothers are often placed in a box and judged. Sadly, these judgements and expectations are not only by media but also by other women. Why do we do this to ourselves and to each other? I feel it can only come down to our own fear, feelings of unworthiness or lack, and insecurity.

Men are not free from this constant bombardment either. Society somehow expects men to be the stereotypical male who is somehow unworthy if he doesn't live up to these expectations or if he shows the slightest vulnerabilities. Often men are expected to be strong, assertive, and masculine without displaying any signs of weakness. The pressures are enormous, but more importantly, they are unrealistic. On the other hand, when you are naturally a strong man, society tries to push you down, with messages that you are not good enough either.

It saddens me to think that many men and women feel unsafe to be their unique selves or somehow inadequate if they were to show who their true self was. If you are not harming yourself or another, and if you are taking responsibility for your actions, why can't we just allow men to be their God darn selves whatever shape or form or package they may come in? It is unfortunate that we live in a society where many feel that they are not accepted the way that is natural to them. It is heartbreaking to think that a lot of men are not able to ask for help during difficult times because of the harsh judgement that might prevail.

If we would only accept each other and love each other's uniqueness and make it safe for each other to let our unique lights shine… actually, if we would really truly love and accept ourselves and our beauty, our imperfections, and uniqueness first and foremost. By doing this, we would not only allow our own light to shine, but we would be better able to let the light of those around us shine brightly in its beauty, power, and uniqueness.

The messages that we have taken from our childhood or life experiences have ingrained in us a deep subconscious message that the light inside us, that brought so much excitement and joy when we were born and during childhood, was not valid, was to somehow be hidden. Although these messages were false, somewhere along the line, we started to believe in them, that we were not good enough or not worthy enough to be great, intelligent, and beautiful and to let our deep bright light shine, which is a part of our core nature. We feel that we were somehow unworthy of even having this light. Therefore, we established the deep, ingrained, and subconscious belief that we are powerless, and we are extremely fearful of letting this light shine. I am saddened that as adults most of us feel that we are unworthy on some level and that our own light, which, mind you, can never be extinguished, is sometimes hidden so deeply that we no longer feel its existence.

I have battled with this for most of my life. Many times I would climb to big achievement, some of my achievements were at quite a young age, only to tear myself down again through self-punishment and self-sabotage. Why punishment? Somehow, I felt guilty, unworthy, ashamed in some manner. But for what reason? None apart from the insanity of my mind – I allowed the other side of my mind to tell me these things until I believed them, until it overtook and held the truth of who I really was hostage. It's interesting how the mind works when a message has been embedded in its subconscious. It is through these false thoughts and beliefs, these false paradigms in our subconscious minds, that we develop a deeply ingrained self-image. Therefore, we continue to ask ourselves:

"Who am I to be brilliant, gorgeous, talented, and fabulous?"

And this is where Ms. Williamson challenges us by questioning:

"Actually, who are you not to be? You are a child of God."

No matter what your beliefs are around the concept of God or if you even believe in God (or whatever you would like to call it – the Universe, Spirit, Source), each of us comes from the same source, and therefore each of us carries within us the same essence, the same infinite potential and infinite intelligence. No matter in what country you were born, what your upbringing was like, whatever your gender, if we were all created by the same source, every single one of us has a light inside us that cannot be extinguished and that desperately wants to shine. It was meant to shine; that is its purpose. This light is perfect in our imperfection as human beings.

Each and every one of us has been created with infinite potential, gifts, and talents. This is why all children shine. They are excited by the zest of life; their souls know that life is wonderful, so they embark on adventure and fun and joy, and they have a deep knowledge of this truth. That is why they have such wonderful imaginations dreaming about being great, about flying, dancing, performing, acting, and just living from their beautiful joyful hearts, until it is taken away from them. Or, in other words, until they allow it to be taken away, until they slowly start to forget who they truly are and why they have come.

Read and reread Ms. Williamson's words until they resonate with you. By allowing ourselves to give into these deep subconscious paradigms that we were taught as children, and by shrinking, we simply aren't allowing our full potential and life purpose to be realized. We are not allowing our deep joy to prevail so that we could lead a joyous life, which of course will benefit all those around us. However, by really letting ourselves and our deep inner light, our joy, our dream grow and develop in us, and by us truly seeing our own self-value and self-worth, we naturally allow that for those around us. How much better would the world be if every one of us were able to let go of our own false negative perceptions of who we are, to let go of our so-called limitations and let our true God-given nature shine? We all have a purpose and something that we were born to contribute to this world. What would you do if you were able to let yourself free from your own limitations?

And please, please remember:

"Your playing small does not serve the world.

There is nothing enlightened about shrinking so that other people won't feel insecure around you.

We are all meant to shine as children do.

We are born to make manifest the glory of God that is within us.

It is not just in some of us, it is in everyone.

As we let our own light shine, we unconsciously give permission to other people to do the same.

As we are liberated from our own fear,

Our presence automatically liberates others."

Thank you, Ms. Williamson, for these deep, beautiful, profound words, for the deep reminder, and for all that you have contributed to us through your teachings.

Afterword – The **Your2Minds** Mission

"Every living being is an engine to the wheel work of the universe. Though seemingly affected only by its immediate surrounding, the sphere of external influence extends to infinite distance."
~ Nikola Tesla

I had been practicing "Letting Go and Letting God" for a few months, so when Bob Proctor was talking that day, I had been open and relaxed. I was becoming accustomed to Letting Go and Letting God. I was fully open and receptive to the message. I had been connecting and felt connected.

When Bob said those words, "Did you know if you weren't here, the Universe would literally be out of alignment?" my entire being was ready to hear it. It felt like the shackles of my mind had completely unlocked and my soul had been set free to feel, to jump with joy, to be moved deeply, to show me who I truly was. The truth had been revealed. My soul had been unleashed, and I was thinking from deep within my soul. It had taken over my body. I felt it. I felt the true meaning of Bob's words. We are all deeply connected to each other and to the Universe itself. I am infinitely loved, important, and talented. We all are. We are all connected and need each other. We all are infinitely loved, important, and talented. Yet somewhere along the way, we forget this. You take one part away, and it is like taking a piece of the jigsaw puzzle away. It is never really complete. If we could just let go of that chatter in our mind and realize our own infinite and intrinsic value, we would allow ourselves to be in our natural state, and our natural state is pure love, it is greatness, it is genius. If we allowed ourselves to see our own infinite value and to be guided by our own beautiful bright light, we would naturally come to know the piece of the Universal puzzle that we were put here to play. We would be guided by our soul's purpose rather than by our fear because fear is nothing to a being that has such a great purpose in the Universe. There is something that you were put here to do and accomplish, and nobody else alive has that same talent and ability. The piece of your puzzle is important. The whole puzzle cannot be completed without you.

Remember Marianne Williamson's words:

"Your playing small does not serve the world.

There is nothing enlightened about shrinking so that other people won't feel insecure around you.

We are all meant to shine as children do.

We are born to make manifest the glory of God that is within us… "

I got it. I finally got it. I now understood on a cellular level that I have a massive role to play. I have my own infinite potential, my own piece of the puzzle that nobody else could play, and my piece is equally as important as everyone else's piece. It was time to let my piece stand out because that is what it is meant to do. I was meant to stand out. You too are meant to stand out. That is the only way we will ever properly serve others and serve this thing called life. Our shrinking, our fear, insecurity, and lack of self-confidence are not serving the world. They are not making the world a better place by any means.

It felt like my entire body had been taken over by my soul. Everything finally seemed clear to me. I felt a big lump in my throat, but I held back my tears. I couldn't get emotional now. My mascara would run in front of Bob and the other consultants in that room. Besides what if I started sobbing… as I previously had the tendency to do in the most inappropriate circumstances, mind you. I was sitting at the very front table. Now that would be a sight: a woman sobbing one meter away from Bob, with black mascara running down her cheeks, her sobbing getting louder and interrupting Bob's important message… Fortunately, with much effort, I managed to hold back my tears. I needed to stay focused on what was happening inside my body. I cannot recall ever experiencing anything like this before. It was clear that my soul had spoken, and boy, was it loud. It was clear that I had just had a strong message come through from Spirit, God, the Universe, or whatever you want to call it. My body felt like it had fully and finally woken up. I was alert, and I was moved beyond words.

And then the message came through: "You cannot go home being the same person. You simply cannot go home being the same person. You must write that book. It is time." I had always dreamed of writing a book and had made a few attempts to do so in the past, but I never ended up completing them.

Completing a book was part of my plan, but I had planned to write it after I had established my business, had a family, and had the time to focus on writing. I had a vision during my meditation that has come up for me over the years about being a successful author, but actually writing a book had been put under the list of other to do's. There were other things that I needed to focus on first before I could start writing again. Isn't it interesting how you put off your dream to do other things that appear to be more important at the time? Isn't it also interesting when you think you have a plan, and you know what will happen in that plan step by step? We try to hold onto our plans and think that they must be executed in that perfect and exact way, but sometimes spirit takes over and tells you that It is your time to do it NOW!

As soon as there was a tiny gap in the training I had been attending, I ran to Peggy McColl, who was sitting at the back of the room. I was compelled to talk to her. I said, "I need to talk to you. Will you be here all day?" I had to act as a matter of urgency. I had to show Spirit or God that I was ready to listen, to follow my intuition and guide, and most importantly, I had to do this by acting immediately. I had to stop that negative chatter that told me that I could not do it and that it wouldn't be good enough. It was time to get over that. I just had to do this. I had to go home an author. I had to show myself that I was worthy of writing something of real value. I had to prove to myself that I was ready to have my dream become a reality.

I can't even remember what I said to Peggy when I approached her the second time. I tried to hold my tears back as I said something along the lines of "I am in Canada for another week. I cannot go back to Melbourne the same person. I need to accomplish a dream. Do you think I could write a book in seven days?" Peggy replied with one big and definite, "YES!"

I did not care how much it would cost for one of the world's leading writing coaches to work with me. I just knew within the depths of my core that I had to do this. It was a nonnegotiable. I had to go home being a new person, a serious achiever, a person who gave her word to do something and who followed through to the very end. I had to go home a woman who had made her lifelong dream of becoming an author a reality. This was a childhood dream. I used to write, illustrate, and make books as a kid. I loved every moment of doing this, and I would show my new creations off with pride. I used to collect books. I could not run the risk of a paradigm of any sort to get in the way. I had planned seven days to see a bit of Canada as I had never been to any part of Canada before, but exploring a new country had suddenly become irrelevant. The only thing that mattered was that I got this done. I did not care if I had to be locked in a closet for those seven days.

When I sat back down, I did not allow any negative or destructive thought to creep up and take over my mind. They could have easily done so as I had just spent a significant part of my savings on having Peggy McColl coach me. The decision had been made. I was not turning back. I had to continue to focus on being connected to and being guided by my soul, my spirit. I had to show spirit that not only am I prepared to listen, but I am prepared to follow through.

Each time a thought of fear or an old paradigm would try to creep back up in my mind, I did not fight it this time. I just kept calm. Instead of fighting it, I gently thanked it and imagined wrapping that thought up in love. I soon recognized that wrapping the thought up in love made the thought relax rather than resist me and get stronger. It somehow calmed the fear, and it gently went away. It left my body. I could not afford to let it persevere. I had become a woman on a mission, and that mission had to be accomplished. I had waited and procrastinated for far too long. It was time to make my dream of being a writer happen.

As I sit here in the beautiful peaceful cottage by Mississippi Lake, Ottawa, I could hear the waves hitting the shore. There had been a small storm, and now there are winds. The fireplace is on, and I feel warm and relaxed. The past seven days have been incredible. I set out a major challenge for myself, one which I knew that I had to accomplish. During the past week, there were moments when I did not know how the words would come and whether I would be able to string something of value together. But I was determined to do this and to know that I was practicing the principles that I have suggested in this book to a "T."

What you can achieve is astonishing when you focus on your inner light, your guide, your gut, and you work on your mindset so that it does not get in your way of what you are able to accomplish. I made sure that I was relaxed and that I was feeding my positive, supportive mind and that I was connected… and the words flowed. Every day there was more to add as emotions came for me, and words flowed through me. I have learned a lot from this experience, but one thing that I would like to share is that before I started to write, before I made the decision that I would go home to Melbourne an author, I thought that this would be a very difficult thing to do. One of the many things that I learned from this experience is that it appeared difficult because I had never fully focused on it before, and I never gave it a go with sheer and utter commitment. Previously when I tried to write, I had been flooded by thoughts that it was not really possible for me to be a compelling writer, so it did feel difficult. Amazing how our body responds to our minds. How the emotions coming from our subconscious mind will rule every action you take and, therefore, the results that you will end up having. Think something is too big, too difficult, or that you are not good enough, and it becomes a self-fulfilling prophecy. This time I was determined, and I was connected to my heart, and that was what mattered.

I hope you receive something for yourself from my experiences and from this book. Most importantly, I hope that you will liberate your own soul so that it shines and sparkles brightly. You are magical, you are authentic, you are unique, and you are one very important piece of this humongous puzzle that we call life, the Universe. Go out and make a difference to yourself and to all whom have the privilege to come into contact with you. It is now your time.

About the Author

As a child, Suzana's father taught her to dream big. Some of the dreams she had as a child seemed to be out of reach for a girl who came from a humble newly arrived migrant family in the northern suburbs of Melbourne, Australia. However, a seed to her ambition had been planted and, as a result, the desire to achieve was constantly knocking at her heart. This desire led her to the never-ending quest for information, for personal development and the study of human potential.

Whilst studying psychology at Deakin University, she was fascinated to learn that we only use 4 to 6 percent of our brains. She was also intrigued to find that 96 to 98% of all of our emotions, behaviours and results are ruled by the subconscious mind. This led her to study the subconscious mind and how we could influence our mind to achieve the results that benefit us rather than hinder us. It was in 2007 that Suzana discovered the teachings of the world renowned Bob Proctor. Having decided to listen to Bob Proctor's audios on the way to and from work, Suzana noticed that her life had began to take a positive turn. She absorbed herself in Bob's teachings and in 2017 became a proud Proctor Gallagher Institute Consultant, she has been mentored by Bob Proctor in delivering the Thinking Into Results program.

Suzana has a deep passion and interest in people and in human potential and as result has a Bachelor of Arts Degree in Psychology; a Post Graduate Diploma in Health Counselling and Graduate Certificate in Business. She has had close to 20 years experience in senior management and leadership. In 2004, Suzana was one of twenty-five international students who were granted admission into Hiroshima City University, where she completed the Hiroshima and Peace Intensive Summer Course, an intense yet profound and compelling experience where Suzana and her fellow students, both from Japan and many other parts of the world had the opportunity to study and debate possible solutions toward a more peaceful world. In 2008, she was sponsored to complete the Ashridge Leadership Processes course at the prestigious Ashridge University in the United Kingdom.

At a young age, Suzana was influenced by her grandmother (Baba Nada), a strong and passionate woman who was born in the southern Serbian village of Masurica. Having thoroughly travelled the world and having liaised with many influential people throughout her career, to this day her Baba Nada, although no longer alive, was one of the most influential and charming leaders that she has ever had the privilege to know. Suzana's love, passion and interest in people stemmed from her grandmother's love for people. It is through this book that she has a desire to connect with people hoping that they too will master their mind and use more of their own potential.

The Literary Fairies
We make your literary wish come true!

Suzana Mihajlovic

has partnered with

The Literary Fairies

Their mission is to grant literary wishes to those who have experienced or are experiencing an adversity in their life or have a disability and wish to share their story with the world to uplift, inspire and entertain through literacy.

Visit TLF website to find out how YOU could have your literary wish granted or if you wish to make a donation.

More details provided at
www.theliteraryfairies.com

www.ingramcontent.com/pod-product-compliance
Lightning Source LLC
LaVergne TN
LVHW011203080426
835508LV00007B/580